A
Time
for
Prayer

Randy Peterson, Anne Broyles,
June Eaton, Marie D. Jones, Carol Smith,
Natalie Walker Whitlock

 Publications International, Ltd.

Acknowledgments

Unless otherwise noted, all scripture quotations are taken from the *New Revised Standard Version* of the Bible, copyright © 1989, by the Division of Christian Education of the National Council of the Churches of Christ in the United States of America. Used by permission. All rights reserved.

Scripture quotations marked NIV are taken from *The Holy Bible, New International Version*®/NIV®. Copyright © 1973, 1978, 1984, International Bible Society. Used by permission of Zondervan Publishing House. All rights reserved.

Scripture quotations marked LB are taken from *The Living Bible.* Copyright © 1971. Used by permission of Tyndale House Publishers, Inc., Wheaton, Illinois 60187. All rights reserved.

Scripture quotations marked NLT are taken from *The Holy Bible, New Living Translation,* copyright © 1996. Used by permission of Tyndale House Publishers, Inc., Wheaton, Illinois 60187. All rights reserved.

Scripture quotations marked KJV are taken from *The Holy Bible, King James Version.*

Contents

Talking and Listening to God

These days, more and more of our communication is becoming one-sided. We read newspapers and magazines to find out what other people think. We sit in a dark theater and let movies wash over us. But there's still one guaranteed way to get a strong back-and-forth communication going. God is always ready to listen to our side, to hear our thanks and our burdens, and to offer comfort and guidance in return. No matter what else might be going on in our lives, prayer can be our constant refuge.

Most evenings when we turn on the TV, we see poker-faced newspeople reporting on fires, accidents, murders, and other disasters. In recent years, they've tried to put a positive spin on their broadcasts, adding upbeat stories about lost puppies being returned to bright-eyed children and similar subjects. But the lead stories are still the disasters. The networks know we're fascinated by bad news. Give us all the details of the latest tragedy, and we'll be thankful it did not happen to us.

We seem to live in a bad news world, but fortunately this is not the whole story.

Twenty centuries ago, the evening news would have led off with a grisly report of capital punishment—a crucifixion. A mysterious preacher/healer/rabble-rouser named Jesus had been arrested, hastily convicted, and executed outside the city. The officials thought that would put an end to the threat of Jesus.

They were wrong. Within days there were reports of his resurrection. The rabble-rouser had risen. His followers began preaching about the Son of God anywhere and everywhere. The authorities arrested them, imprisoned them, threatened them, even killed some of them, but they couldn't shut them up. These Christians had a message to share, and they crossed ethnic, social, and political boundaries to do it.

You know what they began to call their message? The good news. Jesus had died and risen. He had paid for people's sins, and now he led them into a powerful new way of living. For people who were assaulted by bad news then as much as we are today, this was a welcome report.

And it's still good news for us. The loving sacrifice of Jesus has brought us close to God, and his mighty resurrection gives us strength for each new day. Maintaining an attitude of prayer helps our lives, once aimless, to have purpose. We are not lost and wandering around, looking for someplace to stop and ask directions. We are on a journey with a final destination of heaven. We know we'll end up in the embrace of our loving Lord, and that is amazingly good news for all of us on this journey.

So, how should we spend our time? As we seek to live in the power and joy of the resurrection, what attitudes and actions should characterize us? How will the good news merge into our daily lives and spark new ways of thinking in us?

This book provides ideas for how prayer can help us remain in a partnership with God and live the good news as we travel on the path to heaven.

Now don't get the wrong idea about this path. Some religions offer certain principles and actions as a path to enlightenment, to eternal bliss, to oneness with God. There may be some wisdom in these ideas, but that's not what we're talking about here. The New Testament makes it clear that our good deeds alone don't get us into heaven—only Jesus can do that. We trust Jesus' sacrifice and God's grace to pay our way through those pearly gates. We're not constructing the path to heaven, just walking on it. Jesus said, "I am the way" (John 14:6, KJV). He has provided the path for us.

The Bible often uses the term *walk* in the sense of how we live. The psalmist blesses the person who "does not walk in the counsel of the wicked" (Psalm 1:1, NIV). The Apostle John said, "And this is love: that we walk in obedience to his commands. As you have heard from the beginning, his command is that you walk in love" (2 John 1:6, NIV). Paul added, "Keep in step with the Spirit" (Galatians 5:25, NIV).

Obviously, in this Christian life we need to keep moving—finding new ways to please God. Maybe we aren't able to get around like we used to. But that doesn't mean we can't take a spiritual walk as we journey with the Lord. God has promised to be with us at all times and in all circumstances. And through the power of prayer, we are also with God. Our spirits can be very energetic as we honor God and demonstrate love to others. That's the whole idea of this book: providing suggestions for how you can thrive on your walk toward heaven.

The goal of this book is to offer a brief tour of the Christian life and demonstrate how prayer enhances each step. Use it as a guidebook that will point the way to the next feature of this journey. Read it quickly, if you like, as a refresher course on matters already familiar to you, or read it slowly, taking time to consider and digest each point. You might read it with a Bible beside you to check the references, or read it with friends and talk through the ideas. But make sure you read it with an attitude of prayerfulness, open to God's presence and will for your life. God wants to be in communion with you as much or more as you desire God. Let this book help you open up a true two-way conversation.

Rejoice always, pray without ceasing, give thanks in all circumstances; for this is the will of God in Christ Jesus for you.

1 Thessalonians 5:16–18

Keeping in Touch

*Prayer is an ongoing chat
with our Creator.*

Praying is something that religious
people do. Virtually all the religions in the
world include prayer, though they have
many different ways of thinking about
prayer and many different ways of doing it.

Some people kneel, some stand and
sway, some fall on their faces. Others pray
casually as they drive or walk or sit alone
at night. Some set aside a particular time
each day for prayer, while others pray
throughout the day or save their prayer for
special occasions.

Many memorize prayers that they recite
throughout their lives. It's not unusual to
hear adults drifting off to sleep saying the

familiar phrases of "Now I lay me down to sleep." Others avoid such routine prayers, preferring to make up all their words as they go along.

Some individuals respectfully address their prayers to "Father," while others say "Lord" and repeat the word throughout the prayer. Many traditional Jewish prayers begin with a benediction: "Blessed are you, O Lord, maker of heaven and earth." Some Christians insist on praying "in Jesus' name." And many religions, of course, use distinct names and titles for their deities.

Numerous people feel more comfortable with old-fashioned language in their prayers: "Thou, O Lord, hast been good to us." Others have no problem with using urban slang: "Lord, you are the coolest!" Some groups pray in tongues, seeking to honor God with a heavenly language.

Some fill their prayers with praise to God; others are always asking God for what they want and need. Some feel odd about requesting things for themselves but freely ask God's blessing on others. Some pray very specifically, as if filling out a grocery list, while others give God more leeway. Some take care to tack on the phrase "If it be your will."

And while prayer is a common activity of religious folks, it's also one religious activity that nonreligious people do as well. Some people haven't entered a church in decades, but they say grace over Thanksgiving dinner or cry out to God when they're in trouble.

Prayer means a lot of different things to different people. But who's right? What is the proper way to pray? God probably feels the way you do when you get a call from the ones you love. They may call formally or informally; they may call regularly or once a year; they may talk about themselves or about you. But if you truly love the caller, you don't care about any of that—you're just glad they called.

Prayer is the song of the heart, singing in joyful praise and gratitude.

Prayer is the voice of the spirit, chanting in deep and reverent holiness.

Prayer is the whisper of the soul, speaking in tongues only God can understand.

Prayer is the sigh of the body, renewing itself in healing life energy.

Lift up your hearts to Him, sometimes even at your meals, and when you are in company; the least little remembrance will always be acceptable to Him. You need not cry very loud; He is nearer to us than we are aware.

Brother Lawrence

WHAT PRAYER IS— AND ISN'T

Your method of prayer isn't nearly as important as what you're trying to accomplish when you pray. We need to understand what prayer is and what it isn't.

Text continues on page 15.

But whenever you pray, go into your room and shut the door and pray to your Father who is in secret; and your Father who sees in secret will reward you.

When you are praying, do not heap up empty phrases as the Gentiles do; for they think that they will be heard because of their many words. Do not be like them, for your Father knows what you need before you ask him.

Matthew 6:6–8

Prayer is the soul's original form of communication.

For one thing, prayer is not manipulation. We don't force God to do things by praying often, loudly, or with some secret formula. Jesus made a point of criticizing those who made a big show of their prayers "on the street corners."

Instead, Jesus said, you should "go into your room and shut the door" and then pray. Some people have literally created a prayer closet where they withdraw from the world to spend time with God. That's nice, but not necessary. Jesus was saying that prayer is a private conversation between you and the Lord. Just talk to God.

Don't keep on "babbling," Jesus added. That's what people do when they don't know God. They think God will have to hear them because of all their jabber. They try to win points with God—get credit for enough prayers and win valuable prizes! But that's not how it works. God already knows what you need.

This raises an interesting question. If God already knows, why ask for things? The simple answer is God wants us to. "Let your requests be made known unto God," says the Apostle Paul (Philippians 4:6, KJV). In Matthew 6, Jesus added the request "Give us this day our daily bread." Yes, God wants our requests, but why?

Why does a parent want a child to ask for help with homework? Why is it so wonderful when a teenager asks for advice? When a young adult asks the folks for help to get established, the request is welcomed. In each case, the parent knows the need and might offer the assistance anyway, but it's nice to be asked. The request deepens the relationship. And the same thing is true with God. With each prayer request, we say how much we trust God.

Text continues on page 18.

Prayer is the soul's sincerest desire
Uttered or unexpressed,
The motion of a hidden fire
That trembles in the breast.
Prayer is the simplest form of speech
That infant lips can try.
Prayer, the sublimest strains that reach
The majesty on high.
Prayer is the Christian's vital breath,
The Christian's native air,
His watchword at the gates of death;
He enters heaven with prayer.

James Montgomery

More things are wrought by prayer

Than this world dreams of.

Alfred, Lord Tennyson

The main point Jesus made was that prayer is personal. It's not a merit system. Prayer is a conversation with God. Whatever you decide to do about when and how you pray, remember that you are talking with the Lord. And keep in mind that the Lord is awesome, and the Lord loves you.

Throughout Scripture, we read messages that God cares deeply for us and wants to be our friend. The Creator of the universe certainly deserves our respect and devotion. Basically, God represents authority and intimacy. How does this affect your prayers?

Look at the greatest role models of the Bible: Abraham and Sarah, David, Mary, Peter. They all had intimate relationships with God in which they weren't afraid to speak their minds. They honored and trusted God, but they didn't always cower in fear. When you read the Psalms, you find almost as many complaints as praises. We need both of these in our prayers.

TAKE IT TO THE LORD IN PRAYER

Joseph Scriven knew too well about "trials and temptations." He grew up in Ireland, and the night before he was going to marry the love of his life, she died in a drowning accident. The grieving young man set off for Canada, resolving to live a life of poverty, serving the poor and disabled. He did manage to begin a new romance and was once again engaged to be married, but this woman also died before a wedding could happen. He had every reason to be "cumbered with a load of care."

Then Scriven received word that his elderly mother back home in Ireland was dying. He was too poor to travel to be with her. He had no money to send to her. But he could write words of encouragement. Along with a comforting letter, he penned for her the words of "What a Friend We Have in Jesus."

WHAT A FRIEND WE HAVE IN JESUS

What a Friend we have in Jesus,
All our sins and griefs to bear!
What a privilege to carry
Everything to God in prayer!
O what peace we often forfeit,
O what needless pain we bear,
All because we do not carry
Everything to God in prayer!

Have we trials and temptations?
Is there trouble anywhere?
We should never be discouraged,
Take it to the Lord in prayer.
Can we find a friend so faithful
Who will all our sorrows share?
Jesus knows our every weakness,
Take it to the Lord in prayer.

Are we weak and heavy-laden,
Cumbered with a load of care?
Precious Savior, still our refuge—
Take it to the Lord in prayer.
Do thy friends despise, forsake thee?
Take it to the Lord in prayer;
In His arms He'll take and shield thee,
Thou wilt find a solace there.

Joseph Medlicott Scriven (1819–1886)

Prayer is a ladder leading up to God;

for there is nothing more powerful

than prayer.

Anonymous

If the only prayer you said in your whole life
was, "thank you," that would suffice.

Meister Eckhart
Journey in Word

ENDLESS PRAYER

Tucked into one of Paul's epistles is a seemingly impossible command to "pray without ceasing" (1 Thessalonians 5:17, KJV). Maybe you've known people who could do this, usually pastors who preach past noon and still put a final point in the closing prayer. But even they stop eventually. What can this command mean?

Obviously, if your style is to kneel, close your eyes, and fold hands to pray, ceaseless prayer would make it hard to drive—or to eat, for that matter. You don't need to go through life on your knees. Just maintain a constant openness, a regular habit of communication with God through the day.

Text continues on page 23.

Pray all the time. Ask God for anything in line with the Holy Spirit's wishes. Plead with him, reminding him of your needs, and keep praying earnestly for all Christians everywhere.

Ephesians 6:18, LB

Some people pray by checking in with God a couple of times a day. Whatever else you're doing, pay attention to the messages God might be sending your way. And let God know how you're feeling about the various events of your life. If you live a prayerful life, the rest of the path to heaven will fall right into place.

Gracious God,

You know our needs before we speak to you.

You are available to us even when we ignore you.

You are our Rock, our Strength, our Redeemer.

Nudge us to remember you,

to avail ourselves of the tremendous power that comes in relationship with you.

Help us love you the way you love us, O God.

Amen.

Stirring Up the Ingredients

People pray in many different ways, but are some prayers better than others?

In the Bible, people talk to God in all sorts of ways. What should a good prayer contain? Are certain specific ingredients necessary for prayer? We've never been given definitive answers to these questions, but we do have one excellent divine example. In his Sermon on the Mount, Jesus provided the Lord's Prayer, which is more of a model than a recipe. Because Jesus warned against trying to manipulate God with "vain babblings," we know these aren't magic words, but they do work as an outline for our own prayers.

THE LORD'S PRAYER

Our Father which art in heaven,
Hallowed be thy name.

Thy kingdom come. Thy will be done in
earth, as it is in heaven.

Give us this day our daily bread.

And forgive us our debts, as we forgive
our debtors.

And lead us not into temptation, but
deliver us from evil:

For thine is the kingdom, and the power,
and the glory, for ever.

Amen.

Matthew 6:9–13, KJV

Let's take a closer look.

Our Father which art in heaven, Hallowed
be thy name: We should remember the
grandeur of the one we're praying to.

Many biblical prayers, like this one, begin with praise.

Thy kingdom come. Thy will be done in earth, as it is in heaven: This serves as a reminder that we should want what God wants. We can offer our requests, but ultimately we should yield to the Lord's will. Our prayers are not shopping lists. Often, as we say what we want, God makes us aware of what he wants from us.

Give us this day our daily bread: Yes, we can and we should ask God to provide for our needs.

And forgive us our debts [trespasses] as we forgive our debtors [those who trespass against us]: Prayer can bring us back into a relationship with God if we've been straying. Confession is a key element of many biblical prayers. But here we also find ourselves challenged to improve our human relationships. Forgiven people forgive others. As we seek peace with God, God may urge us to seek peace with someone else.

And lead us not into temptation, but deliver us from evil: We've already asked for our physical needs, but now we bring up our spiritual needs. We ask for the strength to stay close to God.

For thine is the kingdom, and the power, and the glory, for ever: We end as we began, with praise.

Of course, not all biblical prayers strictly follow this model, and there are many other examples you can look to for guidance. The Lord's Prayer is wonderful to use, but be sure you're honest with God about what's in your heart.

This is the day of prayer:

Let earth to Heaven draw near;

Lift up our hearts to seek Thee there,

Come down to meet us here.

John Ellerton,
"This Is the Day of Light"

PRAYERS IN THE PSALMS

Another part of the Bible that is full of prayers is the Book of Psalms. It includes many different types of prayers, and you can find a psalm to fit almost any occasion or mood. Many people focus on the psalms in their personal devotional time, but psalms are also often used in worship to bring about a prayerful state of mind.

The Lord is my shepherd, I shall not want.

He makes me lie down in green pastures;

he leads me beside still waters;

he restores my soul.

He leads me in right paths

for his name's sake.

Even though I walk through the darkest valley,

I fear no evil;

for you are with me;

your rod and your staff—

they comfort me.

You prepare a table before me

in the presence of my enemies;

you anoint my head with oil;

my cup overflows.

Surely goodness and mercy shall follow me

all the days of my life,

and I shall dwell in the house of the Lord

my whole life long.

Psalm 23

Although we often think of the Book of Psalms as a collection of songs or poetry, each and every psalm is a prayer. You can turn to them when you feel at a loss for words yourself, or to jump-start yourself into the right attitude to talk with God. Sometimes you might only want to use a line or two from a psalm to remind you of

God's presence and the relationship you share. For instance, the first line of the 23rd Psalm, "The Lord is my shepherd, I shall not want," can invoke praise and thanksgiving for God's many blessings. Because it helps you recall the rest of the psalm, it can also bring on a feeling of security if you're in a situation that makes you feel vulnerable.

Like all of us, the writers of the psalms had plenty of problems with which to contend. Have you ever had a time when things were going so badly that you wondered if God had simply stopped paying attention? There are psalms to address days like those, too. Even Jesus invoked one of the psalms when he cried out to God on the cross. "My God, my God, why have you forsaken me?" is the first line from Psalm 22.

Reading psalms silently, or even speaking them aloud, alone or with others, can help us to unpack our hearts before God. All the layers of protection we use in our lives can be stripped away, and whatever distractions keep us from our walk with God can be emptied out of our minds and hearts. Psalms can provide the beginning of a prayer or its entirety, leaving us open to accept God's response back to us.

But truly God has listened;

> *he has given heed to the words of my prayer.*

Blessed be God,

> *because he has not rejected my prayer*

> *or removed his steadfast love from me.*

Psalm 66:19–20

There is never a right or wrong time to pray. Each moment of our lives can be a prayer when we live from faith and act from love.

TO WALK WITH GOD

William Cowper was certifiably insane. Plagued by bouts of depression, he attempted suicide on several occasions and spent four stints in mental institutions.

Released from one of these asylums in 1765, Cowper made his way to the town of Olney, where he befriended a minister named John Newton (the former slave trader who wrote "Amazing Grace"). Newton recognized that Cowper was quite a brilliant man, despite his serious mood swings. Cowper was also a fine poet and a deeply religious man, though he had trouble believing that God could ever love and accept him. Newton involved Cowper in the parish ministry in Olney and encouraged him to write hymns for the services. (Decades later, Newton and Cowper published a joint hymnal of their work.)

One day, after a garden stroll with his friend Newton, Cowper found a Bible verse about Enoch, who "walked with God." This stirred up thoughts within the poet, who always longed for the assurance of a closer walk with the Lord. As he wrote later to a friend: "I began to compose the verses yesterday morning before daybreak but fell asleep at the end of the first two lines. When I awakened, the third and fourth were whispered to my heart in a way which I have often experienced."

Thus millions of fellow travelers have been able to join the troubled wordsmith in praying for "a light to shine upon the road that leads me to the Lamb."

O FOR A CLOSER WALK WITH GOD

O for a closer walk with God,
A calm and heav'nly frame,
A light to shine upon the road
That leads me to the Lamb.
Where is the blessedness I knew
When first I saw the Lord?
Where is the soul-refreshing view

Of Jesus and His Word?
The dearest idol I have known,
What e'er that idol be,
Help me to tear it from Thy throne
And worship only Thee.

William Cowper (1731–1800)

God looks not at the elegancy of your
prayers, to see how neat they are; nor yet at
the geometry of your prayers, to see how
long they are; nor yet at the arithmetic of
your prayers, to see how many they are; nor
yet at the music of your prayers, nor yet at
the sweetness of your voice . . . but at the
sincerity of your prayers, how
hearty they are.

Thomas Brooks

THE PEACE OF PRAYER

Some folks still feel odd about asking God for things they need—healing, strength, comfort, or food. That would be selfish, they think.

Text continues on page 36.

Do not be anxious about anything, but in everything, by prayer and petition, with thanksgiving, present your requests to God. And the peace of God, which transcends all understanding, will guard your hearts and your minds in Christ Jesus.

Philippians 4:6–7, NIV

While this humility is admirable, we don't need to be shy with the Lord. Paul says that in everything you should make your requests to God. God cares about what we care about. By all means, let's avoid a "gimme, gimme" attitude. But we need not hesitate to ask for those things that are important as long as our bottom line is "thy will be done." It is all right to say "Here's my will, Lord. Show me how it fits in with yours."

In fact, the Apostle Paul suggested personal prayer requests as a cure for anxiety. The paraphrase of the Philippians 4:6 verse in *The Living Bible* puts it nicely: "Don't worry about anything. Instead, pray about everything." This brings us back to the idea of ceaseless prayer we saw in the previous chapter. As you go through your day, every little worry can be brought before God, as the verse states, "with thanksgiving." For instance: "Help me, Lord, to face this challenge." Or, "Thank you for the way you just helped me in that situation." Combine petition and thanksgiving, like breathing in and out, as God guides us step by step. Then, when we present our petitions, as Paul says in Philippians 4:7, God's peace will stand guard over our hearts.

Think of how much money people spend on doctors and medications to fight anxiety. How could they also benefit from the simple biblical prescription of prayer? It's not exactly a miracle drug—"Take two prayers and call me in the morning."

Text continues on page 38.

Alone with God,
I open my lips to speak.
But soon I find no need for spoken words.
Instead, we make connection heart-to-
    heart.
God knows my deepest longings.
Silently, God wraps me in divine love
And covers me with peace.

We are not assured that we'll get every-thing we want, even if we use the perfect formula. The Bible steers us clear of that kind of thinking. Instead, it shows us prayer as an ongoing conversation, part of a continuing relationship we have with our Creator. We find peace in the knowledge that the Lord cares about our concerns, and, as we pray regularly, we care more about the Lord's concerns.

CONFEDERATE SOLDIER'S PRAYER

I asked God for strength, that I might achieve.

I was made weak, that I might learn humbly to obey.

I asked for health, that I might do greater things.

*I was given infirmity, that I might do better
    things.*

I asked for riches, that I might be happy.

I was given poverty, that I might be wise.

*I asked for power, that I might have the praise
    of men.*

*I was given weakness, that I might feel the
    need of God.*

I asked for all things, that I might enjoy life.

I was given life, that I might enjoy all things.

*I got nothing that I asked for—but everything
    I had hoped for.*

*Almost despite myself, my unspoken prayers
    were answered.*

I am among all men most richly blessed.

unknown Confederate soldier

It's the Thought That Counts

God's love can transform your attitude, if you let it.

Friends dragged Mary to see a play at the community center. Mary had been in a bad mood to begin with, and this event didn't help any. First they waited in line for tickets, and then they got seats way in the back where they couldn't see the performance very well. The seats were hard and uncomfortable, and the microphones kept shrieking. Mary scowled through the whole first act, and if her friends hadn't brought her, she would have left at intermission. As she made her way back down the aisle after the break, she heard a whispered "Aunt Mary!" It was her niece

Sharon, a creative young lady. "I thought I saw you out there," she said.

"Sharon!" Mary responded. She always liked her niece and suddenly felt a bit guilty for not keeping in touch with her. "It's good to see you! What do you think of this play?"

Sharon beamed, "I'm very proud of it. I directed it. It's my first time, but the actors are doing really well. This has all been a great experience!"

The houselights started to dim, and both women rushed to their seats. Now Mary watched the play from a different perspective. The seat was still uncomfortable, and the squawking microphones still made her jump, but now she decided to enjoy the production because she loved the director. The actors weren't any better in the second act, but Mary's attitude was. She actually enjoyed the rest of the play.

Attitude makes a huge difference as we journey through our lives. You can greet each new experience with joy and excitement, or you can ruin the whole process by focusing on more negative emotions. It's all up to you.

In most cases, it doesn't take a whole lot of effort to change your attitude. Maybe a quick prayer to remind yourself of God's love, grace, and trust will do the trick. In Mary's case, knowing the director made all the difference. She wanted to have a better attitude, and so she did. All too often we let ourselves sink into attitudes of bitterness, judgment, or fear when we don't have to.

For the Lord God is a sun and shield:

the Lord will give grace and glory:

no good thing will he withhold from them that walk uprightly.

O Lord of hosts, blessed is the man that trusteth in thee.

Psalm 84:11–12, KJV

WILL YOU BE BITTER OR CONTENT?

The biblical character Naomi wanted to change her name to Mara. Why? In Hebrew, *mara* means *bitter*, which best described how Naomi felt at that moment. You could hardly blame her. Famine had forced her to emigrate from Israel to the neighboring country of Moab. There her husband and two sons died. Now she was headed back to her homeland with one of her daughters-in-law in tow and with no sense of how she would make a living. The past was disastrous; the future looked bleak. Naomi had every right to scowl. But that's not the end of her story. Together, she and her daughter-in-law Ruth made a living, and Naomi had fun scheming to find Ruth a new husband, which she did. Naomi's bitterest moment blossomed into a bouquet of joy.

We can find a lesson in Naomi's story. We all face bitter moments in life, and it makes no sense to deny them. If you have reason to be bitter, express your frustration or anger. Say with Naomi, "Call me Mara." But don't assume your story ends there. God may have more delight in store for your future. The Lord can turn your mourning to dancing. Instead of wallowing in bitterness, start looking for things to do. Communicate with God and keep yourself open to the divine will. Don't pretend the sore spots of the past never happened. Just look ahead at the joy that might be there.

Text continues on page 45.

Lord, teach me how to let go.

*I cling to my pain and curse those
    who caused it.*

Show me the joy of forgiveness.

*I cling to my pride and refuse to change long-
    held ways.*

Show me the delight of singing new songs.

I cling to my worries and imprison
  myself in fear.

Show me the freedom of trusting you.

Lord, teach me how to let go of all this

So I can embrace you.

Sometimes our bitterness is targeted. We hold grudges against specific people for specific crimes. Eleanor, for instance, never got over her husband's infidelity. He had left her for another woman, leaving Eleanor to care for two daughters, one of whom had a disability. Life was tough for Eleanor, but it was made tougher by the hate in her heart.

She extended her grudge upward and outward, blaming God for allowing this to happen and being wary of anyone else who might mistreat her. She was on her deathbed before she finally made her peace with God. But what a waste! She spent 30 years with bitterness chewing away at her soul. She could have been communing with God, growing closer and closer to the Creator who loved her. But she refused.

Contrast Eleanor with Lisa, her disabled daughter. Lisa had just as many reasons to be bitter—in fact, many more reasons. She grew up without a dad, and she had to endure the mockery of cruel classmates. But she refused to be defeated by all that. "I just figured those people had their own problems," she now says as an adult. And Lisa was actually the one who helped guide her mother to her final peace.

What made the difference? Somehow Lisa had managed to grab an attitude of mercy. People had mistreated her, her father had abandoned her, and she had serious questions for God about her disability. But she prayed, talking about all of this with God, and decided not to expect more than she had received. That made her happy with what she had.

Text continues on page 48.

*Love one another with mutual affection;
   outdo one another in showing honor.*

*Do not lag in zeal, be ardent in spirit, serve
   the Lord.*

*Rejoice in hope, be patient in suffering,
   persevere in prayer.*

*Contribute to the needs of the saints; extend
   hospitality to strangers.*

*Bless those who persecute you. . . . Rejoice
   with those who rejoice, weep
   with those who weep.*

Live in harmony with one another;

*do not be haughty, but associate with the
   lowly;*

do not claim to be wiser than you are.

Romans 12:10–16

Bitterness is basically discontent. Maybe you're angry over being treated unjustly. Maybe you're just unhappy with your lot in life. But these reactions have a great deal to do with expectations. If you expect royal treatment, you won't like being treated as a commoner. But if you limit your expectations, you might be a lot happier.

Writer C. S. Lewis imagined putting a bunch of people in a room and telling half of them it was a luxury hotel and the other half it was a prison. Naturally, those expecting a hotel would complain about the shoddy conditions, but the ones expecting a prison would be grateful it wasn't worse.

Therefore, the level of your contentment or discontent may depend on what you think you deserve. This is where a biblical perspective might help. Jesus told a story of a servant who owed the king what today would be millions of dollars. When the king demanded payment, the servant begged for mercy, and the king forgave the debt. Then the servant found a fellow servant who owed him about 100 dollars and insisted on being paid, showing no mercy at all. When the king heard of it, he was livid. "The master called the servant in. 'You wicked servant,' he said, 'I canceled all that debt of yours because you begged me to. Shouldn't you have had mercy on your fellow servant just as I had on you?'" (Matthew 18:32–33, NIV).

When you see yourself as a forgiven person, you'll be more apt to show mercy to others. The Lord's Prayer says "forgive us our debts as we forgive our debtors."

Text continues on page 50.

Pray for my enemy?
"Impossible!" I say.
But obediently I fold my hands
And bow my head to pray.

As I prayed for my enemy
I discovered along the way,
It is impossible—
To hate the one for whom you pray.

Forgiven people forgive others. But this principle holds true even if your complaints are aimed at God. Many people hold a bitterness against God for some disappointment they have had in life.

It simply comes down to making a decision to change your thinking. Will you continue to be bitter about not getting the royal treatment you think you deserve? Or will you begin to see yourself as someone who deserves no favors from God? If you choose the latter attitude, you may begin to see and appreciate all the good things God has sent your way.

Do not be dismayed, for I am your God. I will strengthen you and help you; I will uphold you with my righteous right hand.

Isaiah 41:10, NIV

PEACE AMIDST SORROW

If anyone ever had good reason to be bitter, it was Horatio G. Spafford. Only 43, the lawyer had already seen his share of disaster. The Chicago Fire of 1871 had wiped out his real estate investments, and then his son died unexpectedly. Two years later, he and his wife planned to take a vacation with their four daughters to get away from it all. They decided to join their friend Dwight L. Moody in England, where he was preaching at evangelistic meetings that fall. The Spaffords booked passage on the ship S.S. *Ville du Havre* for November 1873. But urgent business forced Horatio to stay behind a few days, and he sent his family on ahead.

Then more disaster struck. The *Ville du Havre* collided with an English sailing ship in the mid-Atlantic and sank quickly. More than 200 lives were lost, including the four Spafford daughters. One of the 47 survivors brought ashore in Wales, Mrs. Spafford tearfully sent a cable message to Horatio: "Saved alone."

Horatio Spafford hurried to be with his wife, boarding the next ship available. On the way across the Atlantic, the ship's captain pointed out the site where the *Ville du Havre* went down. The grieving father looked out over the watery grave of his beloved daughters and began to experience a strange, unexpected peace. Soon thereafter he penned the words that have comforted generations of Christians. Even when our sorrows roll over us "like sea-billows"—and Spafford certainly knew that pain—our faith gives us the strength to say, "It is well with my soul."

IT IS WELL WITH MY SOUL

When peace like a river attendeth my way,

When sorrows like sea-billows roll;

Whatever my lot, Thou hast taught me to
say,

"It is well, it is well with my soul."

And, Lord, haste the day when the faith
shall be sight,

The clouds be rolled back as a scroll,

The trump shall resound and the Lord
shall descend,

"Even so"—it is well with my soul.

Horatio Gates Spafford (1828–1888)

Whenever you stand praying, forgive,

if you have anything against anyone;

so that your Father in heaven may also

forgive you your trespasses.

Mark 11:25

FEAR VS. LOVE

Sometimes we start to worry, and sometimes that worry blossoms into fear. In some communities, people are afraid to venture out at night, or even during the day. You might fear for your financial future. You probably worry about your children or other loved ones.

The Bible says a lot about worry and fear. The first point is that worry does no good. Jesus quipped that worrying isn't going to add hours to your day. "Do not worry about tomorrow," he said, "for tomorrow will worry about itself. Each day has enough trouble of its own" (Matthew 6:34, NIV).

The Scripture keeps repeating this message to us: God is bigger than whatever you're afraid of. "Fear thou not," God tells Isaiah, "for I am with thee" (Isaiah 41:10, KJV). The Psalmist lauds the Lord as "my light and my salvation," adding, "Whom shall I fear?" (Psalm 27:1, KJV).

This doesn't mean the Lord will shield us from all pain or sorrow, but the Lord will be with us through it all, offering support and love. God remains with us whether we continue to pray or not, but frequent prayer works very effectively to remind us of that. We know that our journey leads to heaven and a joyous eternity with the Lord. The difficulties of our present life will fade in the light of that glory to come.

The Bible tells us, "Perfect love casts out fear" (1 John 4:18). Perfect love is not just our love for God or for others; it's God's love for us. As we trust in the perfect love of God, we can let go of the worries and fears that hold us captive. "Cast all your anxiety on him," said Peter, "because he cares for you" (1 Peter 5:7).

When in doubt, pray your way to clarity.

When in fear, pray your way to faith.

When in despair, pray your way to joy.

The Lord is merciful and gracious,

slow to anger and abounding in steadfast
love.

He will not always accuse,

nor will he keep his anger forever.

For as the heavens are high above the earth,

so great is his steadfast love; . . .

as far as the east is from the west,

so far he removes our transgressions from us.

As a father has compassion for his children,

so the Lord has compassion.

For he knows how we were made;

he remembers that we are dust.

Psalm 103:8–9, 11–14

Accept the things

To which fate binds you, and

Love the people with whom fate

Brings you together,

But do so with all your heart.

Marcus Aurelius

And whatever you do, whether in word or
deed, do it all in the name of the Lord Jesus,
giving thanks to God the Father
through him.

Colossians 3:17, NIV

What's the Good Word?

The Bible is neither a dry textbook nor a baffling puzzle—it's a light for our path.

Ken bought a bookcase from one of those do-it-yourself furniture stores. Actually, he brought home a collection of shelves and slats and screws, but the store advertised how easy it was to assemble its wares. When he got home, Ken tore open the cardboard wrapping and laid out the pieces of the bookcase on his living room floor. He carted the cardboard box out to the trash can and returned to begin his handiwork. Things seemed to be going smoothly...for a while. But then he started to notice that he had some pieces left over, and he ran out of the right size of screws. Certain shelves weren't fitting properly. He had to undo some of it and start over.

After two hours of frustration, he angrily called the store. "This bookcase is defective," he charged. "Some pieces are missing."

"Have you followed the instructions that came with it, sir?"

Ken sputtered, "Instructions? What instructions?" In his haste to get started, Ken had thrown away the page of instructions along with the packaging. He was trying to assemble the bookcase without any guidance. You might say that people do the same thing when they try to put their lives together without consulting God's instruction book, the Bible. Who knows more than the Creator about what makes us tick? It only makes sense that God would have some wisdom about how we should operate.

All Scripture is inspired by God and is useful for teaching, for reproof, for correction, and for training in righteousness, so that everyone who belongs to God may be proficient, equipped for every good work.

2 Timothy 3:16–17

Of course, the Bible is more than just an instruction manual. It's also an adventure story of God and his people. As in any good novel, we meet the villain early—it's called sin. The serpent slithers into the Garden of Eden, and the adventure is on. How will God defeat the villain without destroying the freedom of the people he loves so much?

Certain individuals discover a secret weapon—faith in God—that leads them to victory. But the power of sin is relentless. It takes a personal appearance by the Lord to crush the serpent's head. Even then, as in any good action movie, the villain seems to defeat the hero for good, nailing him to a cross. But then the tables are turned. The hero's sacrifice wins freedom for his people, and he himself bursts out of the grave three days later. This is truly "The Greatest Story Ever Told."

Yet the Bible isn't just an adventure story, either. It's a love letter. Again and again, throughout the adventure, God sends us notes about being deeply in love with us and being unable to bear to think of us in love with anyone else. The First Commandment says, "You shall have no other gods before me" and uses the description "jealous." God calls David "a man after my own heart" and weeps when the people turn their backs on him. "I have loved you with an everlasting love" is the note God sends through Jeremiah. God personifies the message through the life of Hosea, who lavishes gifts on his wife, but she is unfaithful. The prophet then puts his pain into words, comparing his experience to God's relationship with a wayward people.

The Lord appeared to us in the past, saying: "I have loved you with an everlasting love; I have drawn you with loving-kindness."

Jeremiah 31:3, NIV

The love theme just gets stronger in the New Testament. Another love letter states, "For God so loved the world that he gave his only Son" (John 3:16). In a culture bound by law, Jesus said the greatest law was love: "You shall love the Lord your God with all your heart, and with all your soul, and with all your mind" (Matthew 22:37). It was love that drove Jesus to the cross. "God proves his love for us in that while we still were sinners Christ died for us" (Romans 5:8). And God's love for us compels us to love one another. "We love because he first loved us" (1 John 4:19). You can hardly turn two pages in the New

Testament without getting another verbal embrace from your loving Lord.

So, as you walk and talk with God, what kind of relationship should you have with the Bible? It makes sense to read it in all three ways—as instruction manual, adventure story, and love letter—for these characteristics weave together nicely. As you communicate to God through prayer, sometimes God's communication back to you comes through your Bible reading. The adventure story proves the extent of God's love for us, and the instructions show us how to love God in return. But still, you might want to think in terms of three very different types of reading.

As in Paradise, God walks throughout the Holy Scriptures, seeking people.

Ambrose of Milan

THE "SO WHAT?" BIBLE STUDY

If the Bible is your instruction manual, you need to apply its teachings to your life. Remember Ken and his bookcase? What if he read the instructions and said, "How true, how true," and then ignored them while he constructed the case? That would make no sense. The book of James actually gives us a similar scenario: a man who looks in the mirror, sees something wrong (say, a huge smudge on his cheek), and then walks away without correcting it. The mirror is God's word, which regularly shows us the smudges in our lives. Don't just listen to God's word, James tells us. Do what it says.

Some parts of Scripture are very instructional, while others need some creative interpretation. Most of the New Testament epistles and Jesus' teaching in the Gospels will clearly tell you how to live. When you reach out to God in prayer asking for help in meeting your needs, you may discover some of God's answers right there in those pages.

Some of the prophetic writings of the Old Testament will also challenge you, and Proverbs will give you some clever tips. When you study these writings, ask yourself: "How will I live differently because of what I've read here? What is God telling me about how to please him more?" You don't need to go on a guilt trip, just see if there are any bad habits you need to turn into good habits.

Many of the historical sections of the Bible describe good examples to follow or bad examples to avoid. With a little creativity, we can usually come up with significant life changes after reading these texts. Abraham showed great faith in moving when God told him to. Samson allowed seduction to sap his strength. Ruth displayed loyalty. Esther showed courage. Saul had a nasty habit of taking matters into his own hands. In these cases, we should ask: "What choices did they make? Were these choices motivated by faith?

What was the result? Did God seem pleased? What will happen if I make similar choices?"

Be careful to take Bible verses in context. Don't build a theology on one minor detail; look for the broad themes of entire paragraphs and whole stories. Understand where your particular text fits within the entire adventure story. This is especially true when dealing with Old Testament law (mid-Exodus through Deuteronomy). The New Testament makes it clear that Christians are not bound by the law, but it still has great value to us. Fortunately, to use a couple of Old Testament examples, you don't need to stone disobedient children to death or avoid eating shellfish, but you do want to consider what God was revealing to his people about himself.

The Bible criticizes people with "itching ears" who listen only to what they want to hear. Avoid that tendency in your own Bible study. Look for the challenges. Don't be satisfied with the same old interpretation. In prayer beforehand, ask God to show you something new. Go beyond the "How true," and zero in on the "So what?" What difference will this instruction manual make in your life?

Let God speak to you. God will want to connect with you as you read, so try starting each Bible reading with a little prayer: "Lord, show me something about yourself in these words." And then end with another prayer: "Lord, help me take these truths with me as I live each day."

Most people are bothered by those passages of Scripture they don't understand, but for me I have always noticed that the passages that bother me are those I do understand.

Mark Twain

When you read God's Word, you must constantly be saying to yourself, "It is talking to me, and about me."

Søren Kierkegaard

FOLLOWING GOD'S WORD WITH LOVE

"Lord, what is love?"

"Love is that which inspired My life, and
led Me to My cross, and held Me on
My cross. Love is that which will make
it thy joy to lay down thy life for thy
brethren."

Amy Carmichael, "If"

Amy Carmichael was walking with her
brothers when she saw an elderly beggar
woman struggling with her bag of belong-
ings. They rushed to help her. But then
Amy noticed the looks she was getting
from passersby. For a moment she was
embarrassed to be seen with this dirty
woman of the streets. Then a Bible passage, 1 Corinthians 3:12–14, came to
mind, promising reward for actions that
honor the Lord. It was a turning point in
young Amy's life. That afternoon, as she

sat in her room reflecting, she determined that nothing but the things that were eternal would ever matter to her again.

A short time later, she was struck by a phrase from the tiny epistle of Jude: "Now to him who is able to keep you from falling, and to make you stand without blemish in the presence of his glory with rejoicing" (Jude 24). That night at dinner, Amy's friends were griping about their mutton chops being badly prepared. Earlier she might have joined in their complaints, but now she had a different perspective. "What does it matter about mutton chops?" she wrote in her journal. "O Lord, we know Thou art able to keep us from falling."

The Bible became an integral part of Amy Carmichael's life as she went to Japan and India as a missionary, always struggling with her own poor health. The assurance that God "is able to keep you from falling" took on a physical meaning for the sickly woman, but it also upheld her in her work. In India, she courageously fought to abolish the temple slavery of children, founding a ministry that cared for these children and eventually changing national laws. Late in life, she continued to help people through her devotional writing, which reflected the main theme of her life—hearing God's voice in Scripture and responding with courageous obedience.

Prayer is more than uttered words. It is a dynamic two-way conversation with Heaven. It requires listening as much as speaking.

PRIVATE MOMENTS WITH GOD

If the Bible is a love letter, you want to take the time to read it and reread it—and reread it some more. Apart from serious Bible study, you need some time to sit quietly with God and meditate on his message of love. For these purposes, you might sometimes want to limit your readings to the portion of the Old Testament beginning in the Psalms and ending with Jeremiah, as well as the entire New Testament. The message is especially concentrated in this middle section, although other portions of the Old Testament also speak of God's love.

In these special times with God, you're not trying to analyze the deeper meaning of scriptural truth. You're just trying to hear God's message of love and respond to it. Read a passage and ask yourself: "How is God showing me his love in these verses? How does he want me to love him back?" Then let your mind mull over these thoughts for a while. Think about how much God loves you. Thank God. Thank God again. Brainstorm ways to love God more. Let your heart become full with gratitude and joy.

The experts call this meditation, and you can read books with all sorts of ideas and techniques, but basically it's just spending quiet time with God, listening to God's message of love, and basking in God's wonderful presence.

May our prayers be honest,

May our prayers be true.

May we boldly share

Our love with you.

Lord, speak to me through these pages.

Let me hear your gentle words

Come whispering through the ages

And thundering through the world.

Challenge me and change me

Comfort me and calm.

Completely rearrange me

Soothe me with a psalm.

Teach me how to please you

Show me how to live

Inspire me to praise you

For all the love you give.

Prayer is not just a time to tell God your needs; it is a time to listen to him, to learn his plans for you, and to obey him.

The Whole Truth

Find wholeness in holiness.

In our world today, many folks think of Christians as "No" people, the sort who are overcritical and always solemn. They never hear Christians laugh; instead they hear complaints about everything under the sun. It must seem that some Christians live partial lives, cut off from the good times that their neighbors are enjoying. A writer once poked fun at a group of Christians by saying they were always worried that someone, somewhere, somehow, might be having fun.

If that's what our lives look like, there's a problem. We should be "Yes" people, exuding the joy of our Creator and sharing

God's love with others. We shouldn't keep all that attention just to ourselves. In our prayers, we should say yes to lives full of good things. Maybe that means we say no to some bad things, but whatever temporary pleasures we're missing out on, we more than make up for them as we enjoy the fullness of our relationship with God.

After many invitations, Rob finally got his pal Carlos to come to church with him. "All right, I'll come," said Carlos. "But I don't want to be all holy or anything." For many people these days, *holy* is a bad word. It conjures images of Puritans putting people in the stocks or nuns slapping knuckles with rulers. Holy people have no fun. They never get involved in real people's problems. They're so heavenly minded, they're no earthly good.

Is that what the Bible teaches about holiness? To be completely honest, yes, that's a little bit of what it teaches. But Scripture paints a much broader scene. When you look at the complete picture in the Old and New Testaments, holiness is mostly a matter of connecting with God, and that's a very positive thing. It's not just a matter of saying no to the evils of the world. It means saying yes to God in all the areas of your life. Prayer is one of the avenues we can take to reach God, but we must also make sure God is present in our actions and thoughts.

"I'm no saint." You often hear Christians make this nice, humble remark. They're admitting that they sin every so often. But technically their statement is wrong. They are saints. Not in the sense that they're canonized by any church, but the fact is that the New Testament uses this term for all believers. When Paul writes to the various churches in Rome, in Corinth, in Ephesus, in Philippi, he writes to the "saints" in those places. The word literally means "holy ones," and the assumption is that they have been made holy by Christ. It's not their own holiness, but Christ's, and so they are sanctified (you could say saint-ified) by him.

Text continues on page 78.

Heavenly Father,

Thank you for the joyful messages you send daily to reassure us of your love and to give us hope. Please continue to wrap us in your care and find us worthy of your love. Amen.

From the fullness of his grace we have all received one blessing after another.

John 1:16, NIV

It is a great deal better to live a holy life than to talk about it.

Dwight L. Moody

The word *sanctified* is especially interesting when you look at some of the Christians to whom Paul was writing. In Corinth, for example, there were all sorts of controversies. There was a sex scandal. They were fighting over whether people should speak in tongues. When they celebrated the Lord's Supper, the rich and poor ate separately, not wanting to share any food. The church was a mess—but still they were redeemed by Christ. Struggling, yes. Imperfect, yes. But made holy by the blood of Jesus. And so Paul called them saints, or holy ones.

Certainly we are called to live holy lives. The Lord knows we will sin, and he offers us forgiveness, but he still asks us to try holiness. "Just as he who called you is holy, so be holy in all you do," writes Peter. "For it is written: 'Be holy, because I am holy'" (1 Peter 1:15–16, NIV). But what does it mean to be holy? How can we do that?

WHAT IS HOLINESS?

Holiness does not mean a "holier-than-thou" attitude. The bumper sticker gets it right: "Christians aren't perfect, just forgiven." We know that we struggle with mistakes, too, so we have no business parading our righteousness in front of others or judging them for unrighteousness. "Judge not, that ye be not judged" (Matthew 7:1, KJV) is the one Bible verse everyone seems to know these days. It doesn't mean we have to give up our standards of right and wrong. Jesus was just reminding his listeners that they were sinners, too. Any yardstick they used on others would be used on them as well. We all fall short of God's glory.

Many people have the impression that holiness is a "Thou shalt not" attitude. You are holy, they say, if you don't drink, smoke, do drugs, gamble, tell dirty jokes, dance, play cards, exceed the speed limit— the list could go on and on, depending on who's compiling it. They believe that a person's soul gets soiled by these unholy actions. So holiness involves staying clear of these activities.

This idea does get some support in Scripture, especially in the Old Testament law. But there are problems with it. In his letter to the Colossians, Paul warns of a non-Christian cult that was tempting some of the people: "See to it that no one takes you captive through hollow and deceptive philosophy, which depends on human tradition and the basic principles of this world rather than on Christ" (Colossians 2:8, NIV).

The Colossian cult had quite a number of restrictions—for people to truly connect with the divine forces, they had to observe strict rules about eating and behavior. "Therefore do not let anyone condemn you in matters of food and drink or of observing festivals, new moons, or sabbaths," Paul added. "These are only a shadow of what is to come, but the substance belongs to Christ" (Colossians 2:16–17).

The apostle characterized the cult's teaching as "Do not handle, do not taste, do not touch." Paul warned them that these rules "refer to things that perish with use; they are simply human commands and teachings. These have indeed an appearance of wisdom in promoting self-imposed piety, humility, and severe treatment of the body, but they are of no value in checking self-indulgence" (Colossians 1:21–23).

Paul was saying that these rules weren't actually helpful in changing people's behavior. They gave the impression of holiness but had no real power. Granted, he was talking about the rules of that particular cult, but elsewhere Paul said much the same thing about the Jewish law. Its value, he said, was in showing us how sinful we are and thus bringing us to Christ for redemption. Rule-keeping itself doesn't make us holy, because no one can keep all the rules perfectly. We can only find holiness in Jesus.

So what is holiness? What does holiness look like? After Jesus officially "saint-ifies" us, how do we live holy lives? How can we, in Peter's words, "be holy in all we do"?

Let's look to what Peter says right before that. "Therefore prepare your minds for action; discipline yourselves; set all your hope on the grace that Jesus Christ will bring you when he is revealed. Like obedient children, do not be conformed to the desires that you formerly had in ignorance" (1 Peter 1:13–14). It looks like holiness is a matter of action, of hope. Sure, it involves self-control and saying no to "desires that you formerly had," but there is so much more to which we are saying yes. There is a fullness of life here— and that idea is echoed throughout the Bible. When we connect with God's holiness, our lives explode with possibilities.

The glory of God is a person fully alive.

Irenaeus

Holy Spirit, the life that gives life.

You are the cause of all movement;

You are the breath of all creatures;

You are the salve that purifies our souls;

You are the ointment that heals our wounds;

You are the fire that warms our hearts;

You are the light that guides our feet.

Let all the world praise you.

Hildegard of Bingen

When we pray, we tell God what he already knows.

When we listen, God tells us what we should know.

A LIFE OF WHOLENESS

*When . . . silence and darkness have settled
upon those miles of prostrate sick, she may be
observed alone, with a little lamp in her
hand, making the solitary rounds.*

The Times (London), circa 1854–1856, about
Florence Nightingale

Florence Nightingale had it all—born
in the lap of luxury, given the best education possible, sought after by the most
eligible bachelors in England—but she
still had no clue about her purpose in life.
She wanted to become involved in a
worthwhile occupation instead of, as she
put it herself, "frittering time away on
useless trifles."

She was not whole, despite all that life
offered her, until she found her life's call-

ing: making other people whole. Nightingale had always been a compassionate soul, and she somehow managed to see through the glittery distractions of her society life and focus on people's suffering. At the age of 30, still searching for purpose, she visited a Christian hospice in Germany and was impressed by the loving dedication of the nurses there. "Now I know," Nightingale wrote in her diary.

She returned to London to take a position with the Institution for the Care of Sick Gentlewomen in Distressed Circumstances. Then cholera broke out in the city, and she coordinated national nursing efforts. During the Crimean War, she oversaw the nurses at a military hospital in Turkey. From there came the enduring image of Florence Nightingale, lamp in hand, checking on the patients. Yet people don't always realize the ultimate motivation for her work. "Christ is the author of our profession," she once said. As a faithful believer, she was finding wholeness in administering wholeness to others.

Lord, make me whole.

Like the woman who touched your cloak for
       healing,

I reach out to you, O Lord.

Hoping, believing, trusting, longing for your
       power.

I don't want to be some otherworldly pious
       person.

I don't need other people to say, "There goes
       someone holy!"

I just want to please you with my life.

Fill me with your fullness.

Make me all you created me to be.

Prayer is a participation in willing

God's will.

Marjorie J. Thompson

FINDING WHOLENESS

Wholeness and *holiness*. The words are related, both coming from the same Greek root. Holiness is a spiritual wholeness that comes from God. Jesus said he came to earth so that his people might have life and "have it more abundantly" (John 10:10, KJV). Paul prayed that believers "might be filled with all the fulness of God" (Ephesians 3:19, KJV). The psalmist uttered this praise: "You show me the path of life. In your presence there is fullness of joy; in your right hand are pleasures forevermore" (Psalm 16:11).

It's clear that our life with God is a delightful and wide-ranging one. Some people may believe that because they have an active prayer life, they've pushed to the limits of their relationship with the Lord. Certainly, our lives are to be holy because of our connection with Christ, but our lives are also to be whole, complete, and packed to overflowing with the good things God gives to us.

When you think about it, sin makes us less whole. A liar forfeits the purity of integrity. A person who harbors a hateful grudge is gnawing at his or her own heart. Whatever sinful habit you struggle with—overdrinking, overeating, overgambling, gossip, pride—it keeps you from being wholly the person God wants you to be. Chances are, the habit promises to make you complete, but it doesn't deliver. For example, an overdrinker thinks that alcohol will solve his problems, but it just creates more. He wants to be witty, the life of the party, but after too many drinks, he acts like a slobbering fool. A compulsive gambler thinks she'll win the money that will buy her happiness. Instead, she sinks deeper in debt. These are just a few of the sins, but they all tend to make you less than a whole person. How then will you live a life of wholeness as you move along your spiritual path?

Don't buy the lies. Reject the idea that sinful behavior will give you what you need. Many of us have a pet sin that we keep turning to when we're stressed or depressed. We keep expecting it to soothe us, although it always makes our lives worse. Whatever your pet sin is, or even if you have a whole menu of them, be aware that you're being lied to. Sin does not satisfy. Maybe in the moment it provides a pleasant diversion, but in the long term it won't make you whole.

Find the positive alternative. Don't just say no. Find a positive way to replace the sinful behavior you've rejected. Prayer can be part of that, but there's much more you can do besides. Call a friend. Sing a song. Walk in the park. For instance, if you're tempted to gamble away that check you just got in the mail, you might plan a shopping trip instead and buy gifts for your children or grandchildren.

Celebrate. Find regular times to celebrate your fullness of life in Christ. This might occur weekly in your church. But if it occurs "weakly" in your church—that is, if your church doesn't celebrate as much as you would like—then add your own celebration to your schedule. Invite your friends and family to a time of praise and prayer and fun. Or just find your own method of celebration.

Text continues on page 92.

Lord and Creator, put your kindness in our hearts. Give us ears to hear the cries of those around us. Give us intentions that are pure. Teach us to love. Teach us to touch. Teach us to see beyond opinions and politics and, yes, even religion if those things keep us from being your arms reaching out to this broken world. Help us to look past differences and see struggling souls. Help us to look beyond prejudices and see men and women finding their way. Amen.

Father, hear the prayer we offer:

Not for ease that prayer shall be,

But for strength that we may ever

Live our lives courageously.

Love Maria Willis

If you pray truly, you will feel within your-
self a great assurance, and the angels will be
your companions.

Evagrius of Pontus

Between the humble and contrite heart and

the mystery of heaven there are no barriers;

the only password is prayer.

Hosea Ballou

Hold your tongue. There are many Christians who avoid the more obvious sins throughout their lives, but they regularly sin in their speech. Nasty comments, gossip, judgmental words, or racial slurs can creep into our speech if we're not careful. Statements like these diminish the wholeness of ourselves and others.

Consider the company you keep. Psalm 1 offers blessing to the person who does not take the path that sinners walk or sit in the seat of scoffers. Our companions can strongly influence us, for good or ill. Of course, we can also influence them. You don't need to sever ties with all people who struggle with sinful habits—you'd be mighty lonely in that case—but do be aware of how others sway you. If a particular companion always gets you in trouble, back away.

Build wholeness in others. You probably know people who do this. When you see them, they are encouraging, supporting, and building you up. You, too, can do that for others. Instead of criticizing people, affirm them. Instead of telling them everything they did wrong, find something they did right and praise them. This is the road to wholeness.

An idle life and a holy heart is a contradiction.

Thomas Brooks

Pray as though no work would help, and work as though no prayer would help.

German Proverb

Do the Right Thing

Discover the discipline to honor God in your daily struggles.

Jimmy had an idea for a painting. He was all of nine years old, but his mother was a painter, and he saw an image in his mind's eye that would be "so cool." It would be the earth, "like it's in space, but with the hand of God underneath it, holding it up." He told his mom about it, and she suggested that he try to paint it himself. She set him up with a small canvas and some paints.

The boy struggled to capture his vision. He had never cared much about drawing, but now he longed to get this scene right. Jimmy tried to sketch the picture first, as his mother suggested, but he had no skill at drawing hands. Then he went ahead and tried painting, but the earth just looked like a blue circle, not a sphere. He found it terribly frustrating to have a picture in clear focus in his head but to be unable to create anything like it. After several attempts, the boy gave up.

With a few changes, this could be the story of many Christians these days. They see an image of the kind of person they want to be—spending regular time in prayer, spiritually in tune with Christ, consistently kind to others, studying their Bible frequently, perhaps even leading others closer to God.

It would be "so cool" to live a life like that, but when they try, it's too difficult. Maybe they make a New Year's resolution to pray for a half hour each day, but a month later it's just a memory. Or perhaps they try reading the Bible all the way through, but stall out in Exodus. They might even put a Bible verse on the mirror, perhaps "Love one another," but by afternoon they're talking trash about the people around them.

Christian living can be tough stuff. No matter how clear the image is in your mind, you still have to work at it. Jimmy could have used some art lessons. As Christians, we need living lessons. We need to practice the art of following Christ. It won't happen immediately for us. There will be slipups along the way. We just need to practice discipline to do better each new day.

It is good to give thanks to the Lord,

to sing praises to your name, O Most High;

to declare your steadfast love in the morning,

and your faithfulness by night.

Psalm 92:1–2

THE FRUSTRATED APOSTLE

The Apostle Paul wrote many brilliant things. His 13 letters that appear in the New Testament are full of powerful insights. But one of the most helpful chapters he ever wrote was probably his most embarrassing. In Romans 7, he confesses that he has trouble doing the right thing. "I do not understand my own actions," he writes. "For I do not do what I want, but I do the very thing I hate. . . . I can will what is right, but I cannot do it." And he continues in this manner, calling himself a "captive to the law of sin" and a "wretched man" (Romans 7:15–24).

We've all been there, haven't we? We've all had those moments of clear-cut choices. Donate money to feed the poor or buy a bag of tortilla chips—which will it be? We know the right thing to do, but we don't do it. And later, as we're scraping the bottom of the nacho-cheese-dip can, we feel guilty. If we were really good people, we'd make the right choice, wouldn't we?

That's why Paul's confession is so important. Here's a guy who walked closely with God. Following Jesus was his passion. He was the very model of "good people." But still he struggled with the same problem: doing the right thing instead of the wrong thing.

After honestly confessing his struggle in Romans 7, Paul launches into one of the most magnificent chapters in all of Scripture: Romans 8. Paul writes what you might call Keys to Christian Discipline, or Seven Tips for Victorious Living. Although not that programmed, they do give us helpful ideas.

1) Don't condemn yourself. After you fail once again to make the proper choice, it's natural to think about what a bad person you are. But that's not what God is thinking. "There is therefore now no condemnation for those who are in Christ Jesus" (Romans 8:1). Your sin has been paid for. Let the matter drop.

2) Change your mind. The focus is now on what to do next time. How can you set

yourself up to make better decisions? It's all in your mind. "To set the mind on the flesh is death, but to set the mind on the Spirit is life and peace" (Romans 8:6). If you are dwelling on the physical desire for those tortilla chips, shift your focus to the spiritual benefit of sharing God's love.

3) Feel the power. In Romans 8:11, Paul says that the same Spirit who raised Jesus from the dead is living within you.

4) Be led. Romans 8:14 talks about being "led" by God's Spirit. Pay attention to the Spirit's voice within you, and follow step by step.

5) Groan to God. Sometimes you're so far down you don't even know how to pray. Good. That's exactly where God wants you. Romans 8:26 tells us that no one knows how to pray properly. But "the Spirit helps us in our weakness," taking our frustrations and translating them into "sighs too deep for words." *The King James Version* is even more dramatic, calling these "groanings which cannot be uttered." So even when you don't know

exactly what you should say to God, at least groan in his direction. God will take it from there.

6) Perceive the plan. God has a plan, according to Romans 8:28–30, and it's going to be grand. Whatever present difficulties might be clouding your vision, know that there is glory ahead.

7) Celebrate the victory of love. The final verses of Romans 8 call us "more than conquerors through him who loved us." We're promised that nothing will separate us from the love of God. Love should be our motivation in our day-to-day lives.

Father, hear me as I pray.

    Guide me safely through the day.

    God in heaven above,

    Fix your eyes on those I love.

Lord, when night is dark and deep,

Gently guard us as we sleep.

IN THE NAME OF LOVE

Tracy was at the corner, chatting with some friends, when her mother drove up and rolled down the car window, saying, "Could you come home now, Tracy? I need to talk with you." The daughter sighed, "All right," rolling her eyes so her friends could see. But a half hour later she was still standing there when she heard her mom's angry voice from halfway down the block. "TRACY, GET OVER HERE!" The girl stopped mid-sentence and ran home.

She was not a bad kid. It just wasn't cool to do everything your parents said, especially not in front of your friends. But as Tracy hurried inside the house to catch up with her irate mother, she felt genuinely guilty, and she tried to think of an appropriate apology. "Mom," she began, "I'm sorry. I know you love me, and that's important to me. And I don't want to do anything to make you love me less."

Her mother, a bit softened by these words, just shook her head. "Tracy, I'll never love you any less. You could blow up this house, and I wouldn't love you any less. But because I love you, I want you to love me back. And I want you to let your friends know that you love me, by doing what I ask, even right in front of them. You are part of this family. That is who you are. And I want you to do the loving thing, not because you're afraid you'll lose my love but because of who you are—the daughter I love."

God could say much the same thing to us as Tracy's mom said to her. In fact, that's what we are told in Romans 8. Paul says we are beloved children of a loving Lord, and because of this we should show love in return. Even then, we will mess up sometimes, and God will still love us.

As long as habit and routine dictate the pattern of living, new dimensions of the soul will not emerge.

Henry van Dyke

Lord, humbly I come to you now,
Faithful, I prayerfully bow,
Earnest, I freely confide,
Hoping in your grace I'll abide,
Seeking to gain your good will,
Yet aware of the sin I have still,
I'll trust in you every hour,
And in your magnificent power.

God answers all prayers. If we think he hasn't heard us, we are simply looking in the wrong place for his answers—or looking for the wrong answers.

Prayer is exhaling the spirit of man and inhaling the spirit of God.

Edwin Keith

DEVOTED TO THE LORD

Living a life in service to God is not a guarantee of comfort. Henry Francis Lyte knew that. His mother gave him an early love of Bible stories and prayers, but his father abandoned the family, and his mother died shortly after that. At the age of nine, Lyte was left alone in the world.

Despite this, Lyte distinguished himself through his studies and turned his attention to medicine. Ironically, his own ill health made him withdraw, and he pursued the ministry instead. He was ordained by the Church of England when he was 22. While serving his first church, he tended to a dying pastor who greatly influenced Lyte's view of life and death. He understood the responsibilities he had accepted in serving God, and he never flagged from these duties. But the strain of caring for the pastor, added to his regular parish duties, took an even higher toll on his health.

Throughout his career as a pastor, Henry Lyte worked until his health soured. He'd take some time to repair himself in the warmer climates of France or Italy, and then he came right back to work for the Lord. A prolific writer, he composed several hymns and prayers over his lifetime.

Finally, at age 54, he realized that his health had become so bad that he was unlikely to recover. He planned another restorative trip to Italy, but before he left, he resigned from the church he'd served for 23 years. He was so sick with tuberculosis, it is said that he virtually crawled into the pulpit for his final sermon. Later that day, his duty to God still at the forefront of his mind, he penned the words to what may be his most famous hymn, "Abide with Me." He set out on his journey to Italy, but he died before he could reach that shore.

The things, good Lord, that we pray for, give us the grace to labour for.

St. Thomas More

ABIDE WITH ME

Abide with me! fast falls the eventide,
The darkness deepens: Lord, with me
   abide!
When other helpers fail, and comforts flee,
Help of the helpless, O, abide with me!

Not a brief glance I beg, a passing word;
But, as thou dwell'st with thy disciples,
   Lord,
Familiar, condescending, patient, free,
Come, not to sojourn, but abide with me!

Come not in terrors, as the King of kings;
But kind and good, with healing in thy
   wings;
Tears for all woes, a heart for every plea;
Come, Friend of sinners, and thus 'bide
   with me!

Thou on my head in early youth didst
   smile;

And, though rebellious and perverse
   meanwhile,
Thou hast not left me, oft as I left thee;
On to the close, O Lord, abide with me!

                      Henry Francis Lyte (1793–1847)

I pray that, according to the riches of his glory, he may grant that you may be strengthened in your inner being with power through his Spirit.

                      Ephesians 3:16

The saints are the sinners who keep on trying.

                      Robert Louis Stevenson

BEING A DISCIPLE

Does all this mean it doesn't matter how we live? Not at all. The Bible speaks about growth and renewal, about the transformation of our lives. We are certainly forgiven for our bad choices, but we are urged to do better next time, because that is who we are—people who follow Christ, people who are led by God's Spirit.

Think of the United States Marine Corps. A mystique surrounds this branch of the armed services: "The few. The proud. The Marines." They are known for their tough training at boot camp, their self-discipline, and their high standards. Yes, punishment is meted out for misbehavior, but for most Marines the code of conduct is self-enforced. They adhere to the standards because that is who they are. They are proud to be Marines, and they don't want to bring shame to the corps.

Christians act more out of love than pride, but we also follow a code of conduct because of who we are—and whose we are. Discipline is crucial for our development as well. Discipline might make you think of spankings or having to sit in a chair in the corner—pain or embarrassment to punish you for bad behavior. But that's really only one piece of a much larger picture. Discipline is a matter of making disciples. You can see they share the same root word. A disciple is a student, a learner, a follower. Christian discipline is the process by which we learn to follow Jesus more closely.

We see the process of discipline in Jesus' interactions with his 12 disciples. He regularly challenged them, taught them, and encouraged them. Discipline is both positive and negative. We sometimes think of Jesus as being "meek and mild," but he often scolded his disciples for being short-sighted, contentious, or unbelieving.

We can expect the same sort of thing to happen in our times with Jesus. There will be moments of incredible closeness, but at other times we may become aware of something we need to change or an area where we need improvement. It's not guilt for guilt's sake, but a challenge for the sake of change.

In various statements, Jesus defined his disciples as those who "hold to my teaching" (John 8:31, NIV), "have love for one another" (John 13:35), and "bear much fruit" (John 15:8), which probably refers to good deeds. There may also be a price to pay. Jesus urged followers to put him first in their lives, even above family obligations, and to "carry the cross" (Luke 14:26–27). If we develop good habits of obedience and putting love into action (fruit-bearing), we will be ready to carry whatever cross comes our way.

One single grateful thought raised to heaven is the most perfect prayer.

G. E. Lessing

Four Classic Disciplines

For centuries, Christians have wrestled with this question: How can we follow Christ more closely? They have developed certain "spiritual habits" with the goal of becoming better disciples. It would do us good to consider some of these.

Prayer and Meditation. This is the cornerstone of a strong relationship with God, because it is how we keep in touch. It's good to set aside a certain time each day specifically to commune with God. You may often feel God's presence in the back of your mind as you go through your daily routines, but it's important to have a time when you put God in the forefront. Don't just talk; listen, too. You can perhaps choose a small portion of Scripture to fill your mind. If you're just beginning, 15 minutes a day is a good habit-starter. If you are looking for something on which to meditate, start with Romans 8.

Bible Study and Memorization. How can we "hold to Jesus' teachings" if we don't know what they are? Dig a little deeper into Scripture, and try learning a few verses to carry through the day.

Journaling. Many Christians find it valuable to write down their prayers and later record the answers; you may want to try this. Or just use a journal to keep track of what you're saying to God and what God is saying to you in your meditation times. Writing your prayers and prayer conversations in a journal can keep your mind from wandering.

Spiritual Direction. Some churches make a big deal of this, appointing official "spiritual directors" to help people grow in their faith. Other churches call this "discipling" and urge people to enter mentoring relationships, in which more experienced Christians guide them. It helps to get feedback from wise believers. They can hold you accountable to establish good habits and make the changes God wants you to make. Look for someone who can do that for you.

Lord, when life presses in on me, help me to find that quiet place where I can pray and find refreshment and strength in my time alone with you. Amen.

Dear Lord, who blesses all with love,
Please send your spirit from above,
And gently guide my willing mind,
Your will for me that I may find.
Help me walk in your paths today,
And be your servant. This, I pray.

Lord, may I be wakeful at sunrise to begin a new day for you, cheerful at sunset for having done my work for you; thankful at moonrise and under starshine for the beauty of the universe. And may I add what little may be in me to your great world.

The Abbot of Greve

No one should give the answer that it is impossible for a man occupied with worldly cares to pray always. You can set up an altar to God in your mind by means of prayer. And so it is fitting to pray at your trade, on a journey, standing at a counter, or sitting at your handicraft.

St. John Chrysostom

Love in Action

Acts of kindness, propelled by love, can make a huge difference in our relationships.

A man was striving hard to woo a new woman in his life. "Why don't you go out with me Saturday?" he cooed.

"I don't know," the woman answered. "I sort of have other plans."

"What could be more important than a date with me?" he challenged. "I love you so madly I would do anything for you. I would climb the highest mountain. I would swim the deepest ocean. I would cross the widest desert. All for your love."

"Well, to be honest," she replied, "I'm planning to clean my basement Saturday. It's really a mess down there, and, come to think of it, I could use a hand with those heavy boxes. Would you like to come over and help?"

He sputtered, "Uh, I-I-I just remembered I'm busy on Saturday."

A lot of people talk about love, but when it comes to putting love into action, they skip town. We live in a world that celebrates love talk. Radio waves are jammed with love songs of various sorts, and love stories pack the video racks. Love is in the air, but what kind of love are they talking about? A feeling? A passion? A certain magical moment? These are well and good, but the true test of love comes when it's time to take out the trash. Sure, love can feel great, but ultimately love is something you do.

For the whole law is summed up in a single commandment, "You shall love your neighbor as yourself."

Galatians 5:14

Jesus told a story of a man with two sons. He went to the first son and said, "Go work in the vineyard." The boy said, "No way!" But then, surprise of surprises, the son changed his mind and went out to work in the vineyard. Then the man made the same request of his second son, who said, "Sure, I'll go." But then he didn't. "Which of the two did what his father wanted?" Jesus asked (Matthew 21:31, NIV). To Jesus' listeners, the answer was obvious: the first son, who actually did what was asked. Jesus used the story to make a point about the religious leaders of his day who talked a great game but did not really do what God wanted.

We have some leaders today who talk a great game. In fact, it's easy for all of us to get wrapped up in pious words and hallowed church experiences and then forget about others who need God's love. We can concentrate on proper doctrine and critique sinful behavior to such an extent that we never really roll up our sleeves and do the business of love.

James wrote: "Suppose you see a brother or sister who needs food or clothing, and you say, 'Well, good-bye and God bless you; stay warm and eat well'—but then you don't give that person any food or clothing. What good does that do?" (James 2:15–16, NLT). Unfortunately, we do this all the time. Every day we pass people who have serious physical and emotional needs, and perhaps we wish them well, but do we actually do anything to help them?

It's great to believe in Jesus, James concludes, but if that faith doesn't result in works of love, it's "dead" (James 2:17). John makes the point even stronger: "How does God's love abide in anyone who has the world's goods and sees a brother or sister in need and yet refuses help? Little children, let us love, not in word or speech, but in truth and action" (1 John 3:17–18).

Speak to me, and help me listen.

Teach me, and help me follow.

Call to me, and help me answer.

Do all the good you can, by all the means you can, in all the ways you can, in all the places you can, at all the times you can, to all the people you can, as long as ever you can.

John Wesley

When thou prayest, rather let thy heart be without words than thy words be without heart.

John Bunyan

HOW TO SHOW LOVE

Let's say you want to show acts of love toward others, but you don't know where to start. How can you put love into action?

Pay attention. This is where love starts. We all learn to ignore most of the people who briefly touch our lives: the girl at the convenience store, the guy who bags our groceries, the postal worker, the toll-taker. Who actually cares about any of these people? You can feel the love God has for you as you share prayer time with him. But certainly you don't think you're the only one God has set aside for love. That same feeling is extended to all the people of the world—rich and poor, healthy and sick, virtuous and sinful. Imagine what would happen if, the next time you pray, you ask God to open your heart to those around you. Ask God to let you see their needs. This may be a scary process—you'll begin to see more needs than you can handle. You know that God answers prayers in many ways, and perhaps this is a way he'll answer yours. This prayer request will soften your heart. You won't be able to touch everyone in significant ways, but you may help a few. Start by simply paying attention.

Speak lovingly. James chided people who were all talk and no action, but that doesn't mean talk is worthless. In fact, with people you hardly know, it might be your best inroad. Speak words of encouragement, support, and wisdom. Remind pessimists the sun will rise tomorrow. Let strugglers know they never walk alone. Let the self-hating people know they're worth something. Thank people for jobs well done and compliment people on their smiles.

Take time. It's a busy world. Increasingly, our most valuable commodity is time. You try to take the time to pray. Can you also take the time to listen, to speak kind words, to embrace, to care? Don't expect to rush into a situation, drop a few love bombs, and leave. Love takes time.

Text continues on page 123.

Take time to pray:

> *for loved ones and strangers,*
>
> *for protection from dangers.*
>
> *for his love that is growing*
>
> *in your heart overflowing.*

Take time to pray:

> *to give God your praises*
>
> *for his grace that amazes.*
>
> *to seek him in sorrow,*
>
> *so you'll find joy tomorrow.*

Take time to pray:

> *to thank him for healing,*
>
> *his power revealing.*
>
> *for peace and forgiveness*
>
> *when his spirit lives in us.*

Be of service. Many of the most loving things we can do for people involve simple physical effort. Can you do the laundry for a friend who seems overwhelmed? Can you pick up items at a store, or even whip up a meal? Can you lend a car while hers is in the shop? Can you offer free baby-sitting for a single parent who desperately needs a night out? Can you work an afternoon in an inner-city soup kitchen or tutor kids in certain subjects?

Give money. This is last on the love-in-action list, because giving money is the first thing most people think of doing. "Good deeds? I'll just write a check to a charity, and that will cover it." No, you need to put your heart into it, and that means paying attention, being of service, and performing the rest of these actions.

Still, money is valuable, and many of us have more than we need. Next time we complain about how tight our budget is, we need to look at the big picture and put things in perspective. We're getting stressed about the cable bill while many people in the world don't know where they will sleep tonight or how they will get their next meal. So give to your church, to relief organizations, to youth ministries, to missions, give to all who are doing good work to help others with their physical and spiritual needs.

People can often sense when someone is in need of prayer—even if that someone is miles away. If the thought of a friend should come into your mind, why not stop and say a little prayer on their behalf?

Loving, like prayer, is a power as well as a process. It's curative. It is creative.

Zona Gale

THE PURPOSE BEHIND THE GIFT

The Congregationalist Church had just received a donation for its Foreign Missions Board in the amount of $100,000. A hefty gift in any year, but in 1905 the money would support a lot of missionaries. Everyone was happy about it except for Reverend Washington Gladden. The gift was from John D. Rockefeller, Sr., head of Standard Oil, and Gladden had been writing strong articles opposing the magnate's business practices. He protested it was "tainted money" because Standard Oil was an unfair monopoly. If he could not stop his denomination from accepting the gift, he could at least make his views clear.

Many in the church didn't want to hear this, of course, but Gladden was no stranger to controversy. He had already worked long and hard to bring corrupt New York City politician Boss Tweed to justice, breaking the hold Tweed's Tammany Hall ring had on the city in the 1860s.

Not just a political activist, the reverend was present to negotiate a fair settlement whenever a major strike broke out. He sought to apply the good news of Jesus to the social and economic issues of his day.

"The simple truth," Gladden once said, "is that religion is nothing but friendship, friendship with God and with man." His hymn, published in 1879, presents us with this thought—a close walk with Jesus, resulting in service to other people.

O MASTER, LET ME WALK WITH THEE

O Master, let me walk with Thee
In lowly paths of service free;
Tell me Thy secret; help me bear
The strain of toil, the fret of care.

Help me the slow of heart to move
By some clear, winning word of love;
Teach me the wayward feet to stay,
And guide them in the homeward way.

Teach me Thy patience; still with Thee
In closer, dearer company,
In work that keeps faith sweet and strong,
In trust that triumphs over wrong;

In hope that sends a shining ray
Far down the future's broadening way;
In peace that only Thou canst give,
With Thee, O Master, let me live.

Washington Gladden (1836–1918)

*No act of kindness, no matter how small, is
ever wasted.*

Aesop

*Fear and lack of understanding can prevent
us from loving our neighbor. If we pray for
his assistance, God will help us reach out to
our neighbor with his love.*

HELPFUL REMINDERS

Be sure to give cheerfully. "God loves a cheerful giver" (2 Corinthians 9:7). If you begrudge the check you just wrote, tear it up. Then ask God to soften your heart. Giving should be a celebration of love.

Don't be bossy. Remember that Jesus knelt to wash his disciples' feet and then urged them to do the same for one another. As you start to offer your time and efforts to others, let them tell you what they need. Don't insist on providing what you think they need. Also, be sensitive to people who feel odd about being served. Perhaps the best gift you could give is to let them serve you, too.

Your good deeds are not buying you a ticket to heaven. Some people get the idea that good deeds are somehow weighed against sins, and if your scale tips the right way, God welcomes you into heaven. The Bible is clear on this point: We are saved by God's grace, not by our own works (Ephesians 2:8–10). God wants us to do good deeds as an outgrowth of the love he has put in our hearts.

You can't fix everything. Jesus made an interesting point to his disciples: "You will always have the poor with you" (Matthew 26:11). All our efforts will never erase poverty, and yet we must keep trying to help. Love compels us. The fact is, you won't be able to fix everything. But you can make things a little better.

Text continues on page 130.

God is love; and he that dwelleth in love dwelleth in God, and God in him.

1 John 4:16, KJV

Everyone prays in their own language, and there is no language that God does not understand.

Duke Ellington

Don't just love those who love you. Jesus taught us to love our enemies. "For if you love those who love you, what reward do you have? Do not even the tax collectors do the same?" (Matthew 5:46). It's easy to trade good deeds with our favorite people, but try to reach outside your comfort zone. Visit prisons, psychiatric institutions, even youth groups. Take a chance on loving people who don't love you back.

He prayeth best who loveth best

All things both great and small;

For the dear God who loveth us,

He made and loveth all.

Samuel Taylor Coleridge

Big Benefits

Love in action brings the benefit of helping to overcome evil. The Bible says that doing good is the best revenge. Taking a phrase from Proverbs 25:22, Paul says that by feeding your enemies and giving them water to drink, you will heap burning coals on their heads. In other words, it's the soft answer that turns away wrath. "Do not be overcome by evil, but overcome evil with good" (Romans 12:21).

Text continues on page 132.

If I could speak in any language in heaven or on earth but didn't love others, I would only be making meaningless noise like a loud gong or a clanging cymbal. . . . And if I had the gift of faith so that I could speak to a mountain and make it move, without love I would be no good to anybody.

1 Corinthians 13:1–2, NLT

Another benefit of love in action is that you're doing this for Jesus. Late in his ministry, Jesus told a parable about the Son of Man (a term he often used for himself) returning at the end of time and dividing humanity into two groups. He turned to one group and praised them for feeding him when he was hungry, giving him drink when he was thirsty, and caring for his needs in various ways. The group was puzzled. "But we never saw you hungry or thirsty or needy," they protested. Jesus' reply gives us a challenge that will last until his return: "Truly I tell you, just as you did it to one of the least of these who are members of my family, you did it to me" (Matthew 25:40). As we serve the needy, we are serving our Lord.

There is nothing that makes us love a man so much as praying for him.

William Law

Lord, make me an instrument of thy peace;

    where there is hatred, let me sow love;

    where there is injury, pardon;

    where there is doubt, faith;

    where there is despair, hope;

    where there is darkness, light;

    and where there is sadness, joy.

O Divine Master,

    grant that I may not so much seek

    to be consoled as to console;

    to be understood as to understand;

    to be loved as to love;

    for it is in giving that we receive, it is
    in pardoning that we are pardoned,

    and it is in dying that we are born to
    eternal life.

Francis of Assisi

Family Matters

Do you always hurt the ones you love? Open your heart to those closest to you.

He was a great, giving man. He had devoted his life to serving Christ by helping people. He could have been a wealthy businessman, but he used his leadership skills to run an inner-city ministry. He even founded an orphanage.

This man had three children who adored him, and yet he wasn't home with them much. There was always work to do, and he was often out of town raising funds for his orphanage. But at one point he decided to take his kids to a professional baseball game. The children were excited. Not only would it be their first ball game, but they also treasured this special time with their dad. At the last minute, however, the man bought a few extra tickets and brought along some children from the orphanage. Imagine the conflicting feelings within the man's own children. How could they be mad at their dad for being nice to orphans? And yet they were tired of sharing him all the time. You can't blame the youngest son for saying, without really thinking it through, "I wish I could be an orphan."

Every family has its own dynamics, but this man's story is fairly common. Often there is a workaholic mom or dad who never seems to have time for the family. "But I'm working for you," these parents keep saying, and yet it's hard to put a price tag on time spent with children. They probably wouldn't mind wearing cheaper sneakers or not playing computer games as often if it meant Dad could watch their soccer games or Mom could read them bedtime stories.

Text continues on page 136.

For as the rain and the snow come down from heaven,

and do not return there until they have watered the earth,

making it bring forth and sprout,

giving seed to the sower and bread to the eater,

so shall my word be that goes out from my mouth;

it shall not return to me empty.

Isaiah 55: 10–11

Some families fight all the time. Parents can maintain impossibly high standards. On the other hand, without any discipline some kids learn they can run wild. Some families share shameful secrets. Others never learn to share their innermost feelings. If your family has these or other problems, join the club.

Family problems often remain unresolved, even continuing from generation to generation. You might be a grandparent, a parent, and a sibling all rolled into one. Each of these relationships has its challenges. You might be past retirement age and still be dealing with a kind of "teenage rebellion" among your middle-age kids.

But we shouldn't focus only on the problems. Families can also be a source of great joy. No one knows you quite like those in your family. The people in your family are your playmates, your nurturers, your teachers, your prize students. They help you grow, and you delight in their growth. Many people make their first commitment to Christ within their families, and they keep growing spiritually within that environment. Through the decades, family members can continually spur one another onward in their Christian journey.

NOBODY'S PERFECT

As you travel along the path to heaven, how can you make sure your family experiences are helpful for everyone rather than hurtful? How can you let the light of Christ shine through your interactions with those closest to you?

Remember that nobody is perfect, and no family is perfect. You may be regretting the mistakes you made in child-rearing or complaining about how your parents raised you. Stop worrying about all that. Accept it and move on.

Lord, I give you those I love.
Speak your peace to them.
Show them how to
Love you back.
Lord, I give you those I love.
Work within them.
Shape their hearts into
Vessels of glory for you.

Lord, I give you those I love.
Surround them with your presence.
Keep them safe and strong and sweet,
And give me wisdom to love them well.

Look at a few of the families of the Bible. Rebekah tricked her blind husband, Isaac, in order to gain an advantage for Jacob, her favorite son. Jacob in turn played favorites with his son Joseph, creating jealousy among his other children. In David's dysfunctional family, one of his sons attacked his daughter (a half-sibling) and was killed by another of his sons, who later led a revolt against David. You get the idea. Our biblical heroes were less than heroic in their family lives. They made major mistakes, and yet God worked mightily through them. Your mistakes won't keep the Lord from working within your family.

You can break the cycle. In the stories of Moses, a fascinating phrase is used four times, describing God as "visiting the iniquity of the parents upon the children to the third and fourth generation" (Numbers 14:18). Although this sounds mean and unfair, maybe it's just explaining the way families work. Today family counselors talk about "dysfunction," negative behavior patterns that are often passed along to grandchildren and even great-grandchildren. Chances are, some of your hang-ups result from things that your great-grandparents did. You are that "third or fourth generation," and in a way, you are suffering for your ancestors' "iniquity."

But there's always a message of hope. You are not doomed to repeat the errors of your parents and grandparents. Toward the start of the Ten Commandments, God introduces himself as "a jealous God" and repeats the part about punishing sin through three or four generations. But then God adds a brighter comment: He also delights in "showing steadfast love to the thousandth generation of those who love me and keep my commandments" (Exodus 20:6). The Apostle Paul explains that in Christ you are "a new creation: everything old has passed away; see, everything has become new!" (2 Corinthians 5:17). God is constantly transforming your life—God can also transform your family. It's a good idea to recognize the negative behavior patterns that were passed down to you and through you. Then see how God wants to show steadfast love and bring about change in those situations.

The power of prayer lies not in what words are spoken, but in the conviction of heart behind the words. If the one who prays does so with absolute faith and trust, that prayer will be answered, no matter how clumsy or awkward the expression.

FAMILY INSPIRATION

Isaac Watts was a smart-aleck teenager but a brilliant one. At 18, he was scolded by his deacon father for not singing in church. The boy responded by ranting about the awful psalms they were singing. The year was 1692, and the English churches followed the Psalter in an already ancient translation. For example: "Ye monsters of the bubbling deep, your Master's praises spout; Up from the sands ye coddlings peep, and wag your tails about." Each line would be sung by the deacon, then the congregation would repeat it.

The elder Watts did not appreciate his son's mockery but had learned not to underestimate the precocious boy's abilities. "Why don't you give us something better, young man?" he challenged. This fatherly push was all young Isaac needed. He rushed to work on the lyrics for a new hymn. "Behold the Glories of the Lamb," his first effort, was sung in the evening service that night and was well received. He then began writing a new hymn text every week for the church. He wrote one of his greatest hymns, "O God, Our Help in Ages Past," about 20 years later. The words offer comfort to those who trust in God as "our eternal home." In all, Watts penned the words to more than 600 hymns, many of which continue to be sung in churches everywhere.

O GOD, OUR HELP IN AGES PAST

O God, our help in ages past,
Our hope for years to come,
Our shelter from the stormy blast,
And our eternal home!

Under the shadow of Thy throne
Still may we dwell secure;
Sufficient is Thine arm alone,
And our defense is sure.

Time, like an ever-rolling stream,
Bears all its sons away;
They fly, forgotten, as a dream
Dies at the opening day.

O God, our help in ages past,
Our hope for years to come;
Be Thou our guide while life shall last,
And our eternal home.

Isaac Watts (1674–1748)

Do not worry about anything, but in

everything by prayer and

supplication with thanksgiving

let your requests be made known to God.

Philippians 4:6

FAMILY PRESCRIPTIONS

Parents have an immense task: preparing children to live in the world. They are constructing new people through spirit, emotions, and intellect, as well as flesh and blood. This task changes as children grow. At first it's about training. "Train children in the right way, and when old, they will not stray" (Proverbs 22:6). Even this verse hints at the changing nature of the relationship in adulthood. When they're old, it's up to them whether they stray or not. You can only push the bicycle so far, and then you have to let the child pedal. When the children become adults, the parents' job changes from construction to maintenance. Parents are called in to consult on rusty relationships or flooded emotions. They offer the wisdom of their own experience and try to get their children back on their own two feet.

During the turbulent teenage years, the relationship between parents and children sustains a lot of wounds. Many people don't realize that these are supposed to be disruptive years. These are tryouts when you send the child you've constructed out for a test-drive. Does the teenager have too much freedom, too little freedom? Who knows? Parents and children are making it up as they go along. If you're still nursing grudges from that period, it's time to let them go. Ask forgiveness. Offer forgiveness. Heal those relationships, and enjoy one another's freedom.

Don't frustrate your children. The Apostle Paul loved to deliver zingers. He'd start off saying just what you'd expect an apostle to say, and then he'd zing you with something new. Toward the end of his letter to the Ephesians (5:22–6:9, see also Colossians 3:18–4:1), he dealt with behavior in the home between husbands and wives, parents and children, masters and slaves (because slavery was so ingrained in the world of that time). He said wives should submit to their husbands, just as you might expect a religious leader to say. But then he said husbands should love their wives just as Christ loved the church and gave himself up for her. In case husbands thought they could boss their wives around, they were given the model of the Savior who came to serve others. Zing! Slaves were told to work hard for their masters and serve with enthusiasm—nothing new there—but masters should treat their slaves in the same way. Zing!

Children are told to honor and obey their parents, but parents also are given a command to follow: "Do not exasperate your children; instead, bring them up in the training and instruction of the Lord" (Ephesians 6:4, NIV). *Exasperate* means to squeeze the hope out of someone, to make them frustrated. The Greek word Paul used for *exasperate* means to stand alongside someone and stir up a tempest within them. Don't do this to your kids—not when they're young and not when they're old. Zing!

When they're young, children want to know you love them even when they fail. They want to know they're worth something. As adults, they still want to know they're worth something. They want to know you love them even when they disagree with you. They want to know you trust them to make good decisions on their own. It exasperates adult children when parents second-guess, offer unwanted advice, judge, make decisions on their behalf, and treat them like little kids.

Offer wisdom and spiritual vision. You'll know when your advice is unwanted. But smart people know their elders have a lot of wisdom to offer, and they pay attention. When Moses was overworked in the wilderness, his father-in-law, Jethro, suggested a plan for delegating authority. Simeon and Anna, both elderly, had the spiritual insight to recognize the Christ child when he was brought to the Temple; Mary and Joseph treasured their words. Throughout life, parents can be examples of Christian faith. Paul wrote to the young pastor Timothy: "I am reminded of your sincere faith, a faith that first lived in your grandmother Lois and your mother

Eunice and now, I am sure, lives in you" (2 Timothy 1:5). Two generations of faithful women were able to pass on their Christian commitment to this receptive lad.

Establish a climate of forgiveness. So far we've been talking mostly about parent-child relationships, but this point applies to marriages and basically any home situation. The closer you live with people, the more opportunities you have for petty gripes. Somebody will track mud in from the garden. Someone will want to watch a favorite TV show when the football game is on. And we haven't even started talking about the use and abuse of the bathroom.

Text continues on page 150.

Only you can clean up the messes that we make. Only you can bring flowers from dead seeds and mud. Here we are. Make us what you will. Amen.

Many homes thrive on rules. If everyone knows exactly what's expected, this could be a healthy start. Boundaries are good, but eventually you'll need to forgive. Everyone overestimates what they contribute to a home and underestimates what others contribute. If you're trying to live 50/50, people will always feel short-changed. But if people enter the living situation planning to give a bit more than they get—say 60/40—then things should even out. Boundaries are important as you don't want one family member doing all the work. But be sure to have a buffer zone of forgiveness.

Institute a family prayer time, if you do not have one already. Perhaps in the evening, before the youngest family member has to go to bed. This can be time not just to commune with God but to commune with family members, as well. It might be the only opportunity you have during the day to keep up with each other and to share what's going on in your lives. Your family can decide which structure works best. Some families enjoy a short Bible reading, while others just like to talk with God and with each other. Prayer can be focused on problems any of you might be having. This experience will not only nurture your spiritual lives, it will strengthen your familial bond, as well.

God knows us, loves us,

listens to our prayers.

The God to whom we pray is personal.

We pray to One who wants the best for us

and knows what we need better than

we know it ourselves.

MAKE YOUR OWN FAMILY

If you're not an active part of a family, make your own family. Maybe you are widowed, divorced, or single. Or perhaps your children live far away. This doesn't mean you can't have a family experience. Why not gather other people without families around you to create a new kind of home? They don't have to move in with you, but you could care for one another as families do.

Surprisingly, the New Testament doesn't say much about biological families. Paul's comments are about as good as it gets. In fact, Jesus sounded negative, saying once that people needed to "hate" the members of their own family in order to follow him. This doesn't sound right, but Jesus was using strong language to say that nothing, absolutely nothing, should hold you back from a relationship with him. In the early days of Christianity, many new converts were disowned by their families.

Christians, however, have a new family: the church. The New Testament keeps calling church people "brothers and sisters," because we're part of this new household. From the beginning, the church felt a special calling to help "widows and orphans" (which may include some who had been disowned for their faith). These people without families were welcomed into God's family with open arms.

Father,

I rush through my moments or they rush past, I'm not sure which. The insistent ticking of the clock on the wall reminds me that time refuses to stop and wait. Help me not to get lost in the rush. Help me to keep track of what is important to me and my family. Help me to share myself with those around me. However fast the moments fly by, help me put all of myself into them. Amen.

Saying your prayers at night is like posting a band of angels around your bed to protect you so you can sleep peacefully.

Accidents will occur in the best-regulated families.

Charles Dickens
David Copperfield

Where we love is home,

Home that our feet may leave,

but not our hearts.

Oliver Wendell Holmes, Sr.

We Gather Together

Is it possible to balance the importance and impatience of Christian fellowship?

On a sports radio show, a caller was complaining about how bad a recent Super Bowl was. "That game was so bad," he said, "I would rather have gone with my wife to church." Unfortunately, many people share this opinion. Church is seen as boring, trivial, unconnected to real life. Why would anyone want to go and sing a bunch of old songs and listen to a minister tell them how bad they are? Lots of people feel this way—and lots of them are Christians.

Many Christians see churchgoing as a duty. They head to church each Sunday because they're supposed to; it's hardly the highlight of their lives. They may also attend an occasional church supper, but they are no more involved than they have to be. A midweek Bible study or prayer meeting just isn't on their agenda.

Other people draw strength and encouragement from church. The services might not always be exciting, but they tend to meet God there. They're always learning something, being challenged, given a new perspective. They treasure the company of their church friends and enjoy sharing their spiritual growth with other Christians in a small group that meets during the week.

Some Christians attend church regularly, hoping to get something out of it, but often they're frustrated and come away empty. They have questions and doubts that the church services and classes never seem to address, and they're afraid to voice them for fear they'll be branded as "doubters" or "troublemakers." They'd like to have a group of good Christian friends, but frankly they're turned off by the character flaws of some of the other people in their church. They wouldn't mind meeting in a prayer group or for Bible study, but they tried it once and had a bad experience. But there must be some way to make church a more vital part of their lives.

WHERE DO PRAYERS GO?

Where do prayers go when they're off my
    lips
Or out of my heart, or counted on my
    fingertips?
Where do prayers go when I'm on my way,
Rushing along on the busiest of days?
Where do prayers go when nobody sees,
And everyone's wondering what the
    answer will be?
Where do prayers go when my faith seems
    small?
To the very same place, one and all.

I will declare thy name unto my brethren, in the midst of the church will I sing praise unto thee.

Hebrews 2:12, KJV

Are any among you suffering? They should pray. Are any cheerful? They should sing songs of praise. Are any among you sick? They should call for the elders of the church and have them pray over them, anointing them with oil in the name of the Lord. The prayer of faith will save the sick, and the Lord will raise them up; and anyone who has committed sins will be forgiven. Therefore confess your sins to one another, and pray for one another, so that you may be healed.

James 5:13–16

CHURCH IS NOT BRICKS AND MORTAR

Do we need the church? Brothers and sisters, we are the church. In the New Testament, church is not a place where you go, it is a thing we are. Peter calls us "a chosen race, a royal priesthood, a holy nation, God's own people, in order that you may proclaim the mighty acts of him who called you out of darkness into his marvelous light" (1 Peter 2:9). He doesn't say you must have a church attendance record of 80 percent and go to three prayer meetings. It's a spiritual transaction that occurs when we commit ourselves to Jesus—we become the church.

The Greek word for church is *ekklesia*, the called-out ones. We are called out of the world to live in the light of Christ. The New Testament also speaks of the church as the body of Christ. If you've made Christ a part of your life, you become part of his body, intended to work with the other body parts to get things done. That's just who you are now. It's like being part of a family. You don't have to attend all the reunions, but you're still part of the family, like it or not.

Since the 1960s, organized religion has been taking a hit. While people aren't necessarily turning away from God, they are staying away from church in droves. Perhaps you've heard these questions: Can't we just enjoy a personal relationship with Christ? Why do we have to get others involved?

Many maintain that their faith is deeply personal and they practice their religion in private. You'll often hear the comment, "I can go out on a mountaintop and worship God in the beauty of nature. I don't have to go to a church." A fair response to this is, "Do you? How often do you get up to that mountaintop? Is worshiping God a regular part of your life? Do you set aside a specific time for prayer?" The mountaintop experiences can be grand, but they are rare. Among many other reasons for going to church is this simple one: Because it's there. Week after week, people gather for the purpose of glorifying God. You don't have to go mountain climbing; you can make church a part of your regular schedule. Just by being there, the church gives you an opportunity to make worship a weekly priority.

The church is a spiritual family, and that gives us more reasons to connect with it. Sure, churches can have the same dysfunctions as families, but they also provide love and support when you need it. In the church you have a group of people dedicated to following Jesus' top two commands: Love the Lord with all you've got, and love your neighbor as yourself. The people in the church family aren't going to succeed perfectly at all those things, but at least they're trying. The church can be considered as sort of a love lab, where people take the teachings of Scripture and try to work them out in their real lives. Not every experiment will succeed, but we will keep trying.

"All right," some might say, "spiritually speaking, I'm part of this big family of all the Christians in the world, but why should I have to get up each week and go to a church? I can meditate just fine by myself at home."

For some reason, God likes it when people get together to worship. Oh, God will meet privately with you, too. In fact, he does when you pray. But the Bible keeps telling us about groups of people who come before God. Maybe that's because relationships are part of the essence of humanity, the "image of God" in which we are created. Some suggest that when a group worships, their actions take the shape of a cross—vertically praising God while horizontally relating to one another. In any case, God has always summoned people to meet before him as a group, whether in tabernacles, in the temple, or in the houses or assembly halls where the early church gathered. Apparently, some individuals in the early church tried the mountaintop argument, too. The Book of Hebrews says, "Let us not give up meeting together, as some are in the habit of doing, but let us encourage one another" (Hebrews 10:25, NIV).

PRAYER FOR PATIENCE

Dear God,

I come to you this day in search of a most fleeting attribute—patience. I try to be patient, but still I am weak and quick to anger. I realize I have no right to be short or cross with the failings and mistakes of others when you are so eternally patient with mine. Please help me remember my own reliance on your patience and mercy. Teach me to follow your great example of patience with your children. Please stand by me and sustain me, and turn my weakness into inner strength this day. Amen.

BOUND TOGETHER

It could have been a rags-to-riches story, but John Fawcett didn't take the route to riches. An orphan at 12, the teenager labored in a sweatshop for 14 hours a day. At 16, after hearing famous revivalist George Whitefield preach, he committed his life to Jesus and decided to become a minister.

He was hired, at 26, to be the pastor of a poor Baptist church in Wainsgate, England. It was the 1700s, and his annual salary was $100, part of which was paid in potatoes and wool. For seven years, Fawcett did well with the tiny congregation, and his reputation spread. A renowned church in London offered him a job. He gratefully accepted. Perhaps his lean years were finally over.

Moving day arrived, and a wagon was packed with the Fawcetts' possessions. The church folk came to say good-bye. Mrs. Fawcett broke down in tears, saying, "John, I cannot bear to leave. I know not how to go!" "Nor can I either," replied the minister. The wagon was unloaded. A short time afterward, Fawcett wrote the words to "Blest Be the Tie That Binds."

The Fawcetts stayed in that little town for about 50 years. At one point, the king himself offered Fawcett a higher position, but he turned that down, too. There was no better place to be than with the loving people of Wainsgate.

BLEST BE THE TIE THAT BINDS

Blest be the tie that binds
Our hearts in Christian love:
The fellowship of kindred minds
Is like to that above.

Before our Father's throne
We pour our ardent prayers;
Our fears, our hopes, our aims are one,
Our comforts and our cares.

We share each other's woes,
Our mutual burdens bear,
And often for each other flows
The sympathizing tear.

When we asunder part,
It gives us inward pain;
But we shall still be joined in heart,
And hope to meet again.

John Fawcett (1740–1817)

Rejoice in hope, be patient in suffering, persevere in prayer.

Romans 12:12

A prayer is nothing more than a person-to-person call to God, and God always answers on the first ring.

MAKING CHURCH BETTER: ADJUST YOUR ATTITUDE

Many people want to go to church. They show up week after week, hoping for a great church experience, but they leave frustrated and disillusioned.

Donna says, "I've been attending church for 60 years, and I hate to say it, but it's just not doing anything for me anymore. Years ago, in a different church, it was good. But then we moved, and we've never really felt inspired by this church; it's kind of dull. Maybe I'm just getting old, but I don't know what to do."

"I guess we cut back on our church involvement about the time our church went through some turmoil," says Jim, another church member. "Some folks left the church in a huff, and the leaders handled it pretty badly, saying nasty things about people who really didn't deserve it. Anyway, we were pretty disillusioned by the whole mess. We didn't want to just leave the church—that would make us one of 'them.' But we sure lost our enthusiasm for the whole thing."

"It's been about two years since I started coming to this church," says Sandy, "and I think there are maybe five people who know my name. The services are good. The preacher's great. But I don't feel like I belong here. I still feel like a visitor."

If you have feelings similar to these, you're not alone. What can you do? Many people church-hop, looking for a different place to worship, and sometimes this works. However, first try the following attitude adjustments, and see if they help.

People are not perfect. Even people who are on the path to heaven struggle. Like Paul in Romans 7, they know what to do, but they don't do it.

Sarah had invited her friend Kathy to church numerous times, and Kathy had come up with various excuses not to go. Finally Kathy said, "To be honest, I don't want to go to church because it's full of hypocrites." After thinking for a moment, Sarah replied, "Can you think of a better place for hypocrites to be?" Many people have the idea that church is where people go to show how holy they are. We know better. Church is where we go because we know we're sinners who need to meet God. You don't take your car to a mechanic to show how well it runs. You don't go to a restaurant to prove how full you are. You go because you need what's offered there. You might hope that Christians would help one another avoid sinful attitudes and hurtful actions. Sometimes we do. But because we're sinners, we will fall short of the ideal. If you keep that in mind as you suffer through the sins of your church, you might be able to deal with it better. Paul wrote this message to a church: "Bear with one another and, if anyone has a complaint against another, forgive each other; just as the Lord has forgiven you" (Colossians 3:13).

The worship is not intended for you. In this consumer society, you expect to get what you pay for. You go to a theater and you want to enjoy the show. You go to a sporting event and you want some excitement. You go to church and you want to get something out of it: to learn something new, to get a blessing, to feel "worshipful."

This expectation twists the whole idea of worship. When we worship, we are coming together to praise God, to please God, to tell how worthy God is in our hearts. Our own entertainment should be the least of our concerns. Instead, we should be concerned about how God is feeling about the service. Are people worshiping and offering excellent praises out of sincere hearts? Are they listening to God's instructions and committing themselves to obey? This may seem like a picky point, but it could revolutionize your attitude.

Where two or three are

gathered in my name, I am there

among them.

Matthew 18:20

"*Draw near unto me, and I will draw near
    unto you;*"
"*Seek and you shall find me;*"
"*Knock and it shall be opened unto you;*"
His words are clear,
His call unmistakable—
"*Come unto me.*"
The only uncertainty is,
Are we listening?

Walk with me;

Talk with me;

Stay with me;

Pray with me.

WHAT IS YOUR GIFT?

After the New Testament talks about the church as the body of Christ, it tells of the spiritual gifts people have. The different parts of our bodies have different specialties—eyes see, ears hear, and so on. In the same way, each person in the church has a special gift to share with the rest of the church for the purpose of glorifying God and helping the body grow. If you're not quite fitting into the life of your church, it might be that you haven't discovered your gift yet.

Plenty of resources are available on this subject, but most involve a close look at your interests, abilities, passions, and experience. Read Romans 12:6–8; 1 Corinthians 12:4–11; Ephesians 4:11–13; and 1 Peter 4:8–11. Consider where your strengths lie, and then brainstorm how God can meld your spiritual gifts with your physical talents to serve within the church. Once you have an idea of your specialty, it should be easier for you to fit into the body of the church.

Above all, pray to God for the fellowship a church can provide. Approach your church anew with an open heart. You may feel a special connection to God as you pray, but this is a feeling that can and should be shared with others. Praying together, praising together, and worshiping together. It's all a part of God's plan for us.

I have been driven many times to my knees by the overwhelming conviction that I had nowhere else to go. My own wisdom, and that of all about me, seemed insufficient for the day.

Abraham Lincoln

The World Around Us

How can we please God in this crazy culture?

The culture has captured us. We are so dominated by media that a whole generation has grown up viewing reality on a screen. Young and old alike have fallen prey to the culture's demands. We are told what to eat, drink, wear, and drive. Advertisers carefully create our desires, and then companies sell us products that keep us wanting more.

Have you watched TV talk shows lately? These are now the pulpits of our culture, and they preach a strange message. The gods of this new religion are beauty, youth, pleasure, and self-love. Absent from this newfangled faith are subjects like repentance, sacrifice, loyalty, and honor.

You can't say we weren't warned. Jesus told his disciples that the world would hate them because they would never really belong to the world. Later John echoed this teaching in a letter: "Do not love the world or the things in the world. . . . For all that is in the world—the desire of the flesh, the desire of the eyes, the pride in riches—comes not from the Father but from the world" (1 John 2:15–16).

The Greek word for world is *cosmos*. We think of this word as referring to outer space, but *cosmos* actually means "the arrangement" or "the pattern," based on the Greek belief that the universe (including the earth) is the ultimate arrangement. You can also see the connection with the word *cosmetic*. Cosmetics arrange a person's appearance. But when Jesus and John use the word *world,* it takes on an even more interesting meaning, conveying that the world is not just the people who live on earth but also the whole arrangement of ideas and morals and priorities that develop. It could actually be translated as "the culture."

During the Last Supper, in his conversation with his disciples, Jesus went on and on about the cosmos: "If the world hates you, keep in mind that it hated me first. . . . You do not belong to the world. . . . In this world you will have trouble. But take heart! I have overcome the world (John 15:18–19, 16:33, NIV). If this was the sum total of the Bible's teaching about the world, we should all move to caves in New Mexico. How could we continue to live in a world that hates Jesus? Jesus answers this in his prayer, when he specifically says, "I am not asking you to take them out of the world, but I ask you to protect them from the evil one" (John 17:15).

Paul made a similar point when he warned against spending time with immoral people who could lead you astray. "I have written you in my letter not to associate with sexually immoral people— not at all meaning the people of this world who are immoral.... In that case you would have to leave this world" (1 Corinthians 5:9–10, NIV). This is the situation Jesus spoke of in his parable of the wheat and weeds. "Let both of them grow together until the harvest," the master ordered (Matthew 13:30).

So here we are—the wheat among the weeds. We can expect the culture around us to have completely different priorities, but we need to remain true to our own beliefs. Why? We get a good clue in the well-known verse "For God so loved the world that he gave his only Son" (John 3:16). This tells us God isn't giving up on this cosmos; God still wants to redeem it.

As you look around, you see different kinds of Christians. Some have declared war on the world. They remove themselves from all interactions with unbelievers, or at least as many as possible. Their lives revolve around their churches and their Christian friends. They send their children to Christian schools, listen to Christian music, and fight for Christian causes.

There is some wisdom in avoiding the ways of the world, but some people take it too far. They are all judgment and no redemption. They have forgotten how to show God's love to the world.

At the other end of the spectrum are those Christians who shrug off the whole issue. "What's wrong with the world? I've got to stay current with what's happening. The culture isn't that bad." These people completely ignore the drumbeat of false worship that underscores modern life: Beauty-Youth-Pleasure-Self, Beauty-Youth-Pleasure-Self. . . . And soon they themselves are paying homage to these idols: buying things they don't really need instead of investing their money in helping people; divorcing a long-time spouse in favor of someone younger and better look-ing; or taking a job that pays more but will steal their soul. Be aware: The world can worm its way into your priorities if you're not careful.

Think about which side you are on. Have you forgotten God's love for the world? Do you love the things of the world too much? Or have you found a middle ground, living graciously in this world as a foreigner from a heavenly country?

Lord, you give me so many riches; forgive me if I sometimes seem ungrateful. I know you want only the best for all of your children. Help me to remember to give you thanks and to trust you with a childlike heart. Amen.

Prayer is the burden of a sigh,

the falling of a tear,

the upward glancing of an eye,

when none but God is near.

James Montgomery

THE CULTURE GOD CREATED

In the beginning, God created the heavens and the earth. After each day of creation, God evaluated this work. "Good," God said proudly, gazing at the firmament, the sun and moon, the plants. On the sixth day, God made humans in God's image, male and female. Now God looked at all the creatures and said, "Very good."

What does it mean to be made in God's image? We don't know for sure. Various theories have been put forth—we are creative, relational, or in authority over the earth. In any case, there is something "very good" about humanity as God made it. The story goes on. As early as Genesis 3, we slam into the problem: sin. Adam and Eve eat the forbidden fruit and get bounced from the Garden of Eden. Cain murders Abel. And things become so bad in Noah's day that God decides to start over.

But our first real glimpse of human culture comes with the Tower of Babel.

God had asked people to "fill the earth," but these builders had other plans. "Come, let us build ourselves a city," they said, "and a tower with its top in the heavens, and let us make a name for ourselves; otherwise we shall be scattered abroad upon the face of the whole earth" (Genesis 11:4). You might say this was the beginning of the cosmos, the arrangement of attitudes that were arrayed against God.

We've been building our Babels ever since. Throughout the ages, human society has been constructed on self-interest, pride, and pleasure. Every so often, the old "image of God" within us comes poking through the surface. Abraham hears God's voice in the din of Babylon. Ruth senses that Naomi worships a true God. King Darius realizes that the God who saved Daniel from the lions might be worth paying attention to.

The Bible is full of this back-and-forth. Will people allow the true God to awake their souls, to make them into the kind of people God always wanted them to be? Or will they harden their hearts and follow the ways of pride and pleasure? Paul says that God writes his story in the pages of creation, so that everyone has a chance to respond. But sadly most people have "exchanged the truth about God for a lie and worshiped and served the creature rather than the Creator" (Romans 1:25).

As Christians we want to keep wooing people on God's behalf. We want to tell them the truth about the Lord we love. We want to fan that spark of God's image within them, to explain that the only way to be all they can be is to connect with their Maker. But we also know that the world can woo us. A man named Demas was a trusted associate of the Apostle Paul, but we read the bad news in a late letter: "Demas, in love with this present world, has deserted me" (2 Timothy 4:10). We don't want to be deserters.

Prayer opens the door to peace.

But stronger still, in earth and air,
And in the sea, the man of pray'r;
And far beneath the tide;
And in the seat to faith assigned,
Where ask is have, where seek is find,
Where knock is open wide.

Christopher Smart

WORKING IN THE WORLD

February 17, 1877—On this sweet, eventful day in which, with every hour of study, my Bible has grown dearer, I take, as my life-motto henceforth, humbly asking God's grace that I may measure up to it, this wonderful passage from Paul: "And whatsoever ye do in word or deed, do all in the name of the Lord Jesus."

Notation in Frances Willard's Bible

When she was a child, Frances Willard won the nickname "the little infidel," because she always questioned the way things were. "I consider myself an inquirer," she replied. This feisty spirit led her to become one of the key political figures of the late 1800s. At age 31, she was already a college president, but soon she became involved with the Women's Christian Temperance Union, fighting the evils of alcohol. Today the idea of "prohibition" has a bad connotation, but alcoholism was a major social ill in those days, even worse than it is now.

Willard, however, cared about more than alcohol consumption. The temperance movement was a women's movement, and she soon began fighting for women's rights—especially the right to vote—with equal fervor. At first, the other temperance workers didn't go along with her broader agenda, and in 1876 the discouraged activist broke with the movement. But her note and quotation of Colossians 3:17 that she wrote in her Bible signaled a spiritual boost. Scripture urged believers to work courageously in Christ's name, and Willard took the challenge. Not only did she get involved with the revivals of evangelist D. L. Moody, but she also reconnected with the Women's Christian Temperance Union, serving as president for 16 years.

She was able to organize the political power of women in the United States as no one had done before. Think what you will about the Eighteenth Amendment (Prohibition), but Frances Willard was a powerful force behind the Nineteenth Amendment (women's right to vote). She stepped forward to change her world in the name of Jesus.

The prayer of the righteous is powerful and effective.

James 5:16

My Prayers

I imagine my prayers to be winged
   creatures,
Able to fly to the very ears of God.
I imagine my prayers to be mighty
   warriors,
Able to stand against any foe.
I imagine my prayers to be lovely wild
   things,
Tamed only at the hands of God.
I imagine my prayers to be childlike
   whispers,
That no father could ignore.

*Speak, move, act in peace, as if you were in
prayer. In truth, this is prayer.*

François de Salignac de La Mothe-Fénelon

THE UNKNOWN GOD

In his ministry, Paul followed a certain strategy. In each new town, he would find the local synagogue and visit there. As a famous rabbi, he would be invited to speak. He would talk about Jesus, preaching from the Hebrew Scriptures. But in Acts 17 we find Paul in Athens, which apparently didn't have a strong Jewish population. He was invited to speak before a council of Greek philosophers who didn't know or care about the Hebrew Scriptures. He was very much in "the world."

Paul saw and talked about a shrine dedicated to an "Unknown God." (Some think it was put up with the shrines to all the other gods in case they missed one.) "What therefore you worship as unknown, this I proclaim to you," Paul said (Acts 17:23). He proceeded to talk about the one God who created the universe. Paul even quoted some Greek poets who had written about a divine force: "In him we live and move and have our being" (Acts 17:28). Instead of telling them how far they were from God, he was saying how close they were. He fanned the spark of God's image within them. They had devoted their lives to exploring the truth about everything—now Paul used their own research to talk about the true God.

Paul's message in Athens serves as a great example for us. As we interact with those in the world around us, can we use their own explorations to bring them closer to God? It might take some creativity, but it's worth the effort.

Prayer is a powerful thing, for God has bound and tied himself thereto. None can believe how powerful prayer is, and what it is able to effect, but those who have learned it by experience.

Martin Luther

WHAT CAN WE DO IN THE WORLD?

As we travel along our road to heaven, how should we deal with our culture? Here is a brief summary.

Don't buy the lies. Your TV is lying to you every day. The same with movies, magazines, music, billboards—you name it. You are constantly getting messages stating all that matters is beauty, youth, pleasure, and self. These are the idols of the age, and they are false gods. You can't avoid these messages, but you can recognize they're lying to you.

Love the world with God's love. Don't fall in love with the things of the world, but love the people. Look for the image of God in everyone you meet. Keep calling upon people to be the people God created them to be.

Look for the "unknown gods" and wise poets. What disguises may God wear these days? What ideas or attitudes are people worshiping that could ultimately lead

them to God? How about love? Can we
use our culture's fascination with romantic
love to explain the God who is love? How
about freedom or truth? Pay attention to
what songwriters and moviemakers are
saying about these and other subjects.

Spirit of Christ, consecrate the scenes in which
*   I move.*

Consecrate the lonely hilltop where my soul
*   communes with nature;*

consecrate the crowded thoroughfare where I
*   meet the company of other people;*

reveal to me the holiness of common things.

Teach me the sacredness of what I call secular.

Show me the sacramental glory of the lily of
*   the field.*

*Open my eyes to the divine wonder of that
universe whose miracles I have
forgotten.*

*Tell me again that the heavens declare your
glory,*

that the earth is full of your goodness,

that the tempest itself is the echo of your voice.

*Tell me above all that your voice speaks to me
through the heart of my brother or
sister,*

*that now you send your messages not by angels
but by human souls.*

**Keep praying, but be thankful that God's
answers are wiser than your prayers.**

William Culbertson

Contributors

Randy Peterson is a freelance writer and editor who has contributed to more than 20 books and a wide variety of magazines, including *Christian History*. He is the co-author of *Jesus: His Life and Times*.

Anne Broyles is a co-pastor who leads retreats on a variety of topics, such as family and women's spirituality. She is the author of a number of articles and books, including *Meeting God Through Worship* and *Journaling: A Spirit Journey*.

June Eaton is a writer and teacher who has published stories and articles in more than 50 Christian publications. She has also contributed to several books, including *Heartwarmers: Moms Are the Best* and *Charming Expressions: Angels*.

Marie D. Jones is an ordained minister and is widely published in books and magazines. She has contributed to *Mother's Daily Prayer Book, Bless This Marriage,* and *Simple Wisdom*.

Carol Smith is an inspirational writer with an M.A. in religious education. She has contributed to several religious books, including *Angels Watching Over Us* and *Angels: Heavenly Blessings*.

Natalie Walker Whitlock is a freelance writer whose work has appeared in *Family Fun* and *Woman's Day* magazines. She was the co-author of *Silver Linings: Friends* and a contributor to *Angels Watching Over Us*.